R. V. DENENBERG is a national affairs editor at the
Sunday *New York Times*. Born in 1942, he was
educated at Cornell University, Stanford University,
the Graduate Center of the City University of New
York, and Cambridge University. He has been a
United States Supreme Court correspondent for
Newsday, a consultant to the Ford Foundation and a
lecturer in politics at the University of Wales, Swansea, where he taught courses in American government
and constitutional law.

Mr Denenberg has received the Public Affairs Fellowship of the American Political Science Association and
the Winston Churchill Travelling Fellowship of the
English-Speaking Union. He has contributed many
articles to popular and scholarly journals, including the
Cambridge Law Review, the *Modern Law Review* and
the *International and Comparative Law Quarterly*.

Understanding American Politics

R. V. DENENBERG

Fontana/Collins

First published in Fontana 1976
Copyright © R. V. Denenberg 1976
Set in 10 pt Monotype Plantin
Made and printed in Great Britain by
William Collins Sons & Co. Ltd, Glasgow

Contents

Preface

This book is intended to serve as an introduction primarily for non-Americans to the politics and government of the United States. Most of the available introductory volumes are written for Americans and assume that the reader has the background knowledge of national politics that one absorbs by growing up in a country and going to school there. This book makes no such assumptions. I have tried to stand back a bit from my own country to see what in its political institutions and behaviour would seem most striking, puzzling or amusing to someone from another political culture. Acting as a guide for the non-American observer, I have attempted to explain as simply as possible the meaning of these quaint customs and rituals.

In trying to make American politics as clear as possible, I have considered brevity an ally rather than an enemy. The book omits a vast amount of factual material, details and qualifications in the interest of presenting an uncluttered over-view. Some subtleties have been lost, no doubt, but the book should arm the reader with a perspective and framework which he can flesh out, if he wishes, by further reading.

Like all perspectives, mine is probably skewed a good deal by personal values and judgements, and I should caution the reader that not all students of American politics would agree with some of the statements that I have made. Nevertheless, I see no way to help others make sense out of a complex subject except to explain to them how it makes sense to me.

I have had the salutary experience of defending the propositions in this book, in the first instance, against the critical assaults of my wife, Tia Schneider Denenberg, whose sharp eye helped to spot any complacency that crept into the manuscript. I am also indebted to her parents, Lillian and

Sidney Schneider, not only for rearing this discerning reader but also for furnishing me with a congenial place in which to write. In addition, I would like to thank my own parents, Morris and Betty Denenberg, for their encouragement.

I have profited greatly in preparing the book from discussions with students at the University College of Swansea, where I lectured from 1971 to 1973. From them I learned that it is more rewarding to know the right questions than the right answers.

I am grateful to the following persons for their comments and suggestions: R. N. Gooderson, Reader in English Law, University of Cambridge; Frank Stacey, Professor of Politics, University of Nottingham; J. E. Spence, Professor of Politics, University of Leicester; Graham Zellick, Lecturer in Law, Queen Mary College, London; Malcolm Dean of the *Guardian*; Michael Sigall, Professor of Political Science, Wagner College, New York; Theodore J. Lowi, John L. Senior Professor of American Institutions, Cornell University, Ithaca, New York; Michael Malbin of the *National Journal*, Washington, D.C.; and State Senator Alan D. Sisitsky of Massachusetts. The responsibility for any errors is, of course, mine.

R.V.D.

1 Introduction

The American system of government has always held a peculiar fascination for the foreign observer. The New World symbolized regeneration, and to its political institutions the men of the Old World turned for a glimpse of the future. After visiting the United States in 1832, Alexis de Tocqueville, a French aristocrat, declared: 'I saw in America more than America . . . it was the shape of democracy itself which I sought; its inclinations, character, prejudices, and passions; I wanted to understand it so as at least to know what we have to fear or hope there from.' In 1888, a British traveller, Lord Bryce, gave his fellow Europeans a progress report on America, which by then had quadrupled in population from the fifteen million of de Tocqueville's time. American institutions, said Bryce, intrigued the world because 'they represent an experiment in the rule of the multitude, tried on a scale unprecedentedly vast, and the results of which every one is concerned to watch . . . [They] are believed to disclose and display the type of institutions towards which, as by a law of fate, the rest of civilized mankind are forced to move . . .'

Although it is now 200 years old, rather a long time for an experiment, the American adventure in democratic government still excites a certain curiosity. America, obviously, is not quite like any other country. Its geography, economy, social composition, mores and customs are so distinctive that, arguably, any lessons about self-government that might be learned would be of little practical importance beyond its borders. But to many, America is a metaphor for humanity; if America, with all its natural advantages, cannot make a go of it, no one can. Even its endemic social problems seem to have a universal meaning. The Swedish sociologist, Gunnar Myrdal, has predicted that if America succeeded in fully integrating the black man into democratic society 'all mankind would be given faith again – it would have reason to believe that peace, progress and order are feasible'.

There are, of course, other democracies which might serve as paragons, but all of them were derived from feudal or monarchical states. America was a *tabula rasa*. As the 'first new nation', the first colony to forcibly break with the motherland, it established a state where no state had existed before. To the scores of new nations which have been born since then, America remains in some sense the model of a colonial revolution brought to fruition.

America, moreover, was founded in the name of a set of ideals: democracy, political and legal equality, and individual freedom. How true a nation remains to its founding ideals, while increasing enormously in physical size and population, and while undergoing vast industrialization and urbanization, is a question of unending interest. Even if the world were not concerned about its ideals, America, with missionary zeal, has sought to make the world interested. America would be, its early settlers hoped, 'as a city upon a hill', an example which the rest of humanity would aspire to emulate. Their posterity have believed, not without some presumptuousness but nevertheless firmly, that America could teach the world to cherish these same values.

Because of the position of international leadership which fell to it at the close of the Second World War, America has had more than ample opportunity to proselytize. And, as champion of the 'Free World', it has given its friends and enemies good reason to study its political institutions. The domestic sources of foreign policy are not necessarily obscure or inaccessible to the non-American, but a sophisticated understanding requires an appreciation of the political system as a whole. A key question today – which troubles Americans as well – is whether these institutions are being corrupted by the exercise of world power. The 'imperial Presidency', as Professor Arthur M. Schlesinger has termed it, may presage the same erosion of republican institutions that Rome suffered in the acquisition of empire.

Chief among these institutions is a written constitution which serves as the oracular source of governmental power and the limits upon it. Elsewhere, constitutions have had a way of being ignored or abolished when inconvenient. But the essential prescriptions of this document have commanded obedience for two centuries. It has persevered through domestic and foreign crises with a Bill of Rights that has grown continually stronger and more firmly entrenched. The endurance of this constitutional structure, based upon federalism and upon separation of legislative, executive and judicial functions, reveals much about the possibilities of establishing a government at once powerful and yet limited in its ability to encroach upon the citizen's liberties.

It should not, however, be thought that the system of government is fossilized. Americans themselves are wont to regard their original political institutions as the consummation of human inventiveness and the proper object of patriotic veneration. For that reason, they are ordinarily blind to the fact that these institutions are constantly evolving, as much by usage as by design, and that this very trait of flexibility has helped to preserve them.

A careful distinction is made in America between political institutions and those who man them. Although the institutions are worshipped, the occupational title of 'politician' often as not serves as a term of opprobrium. That the people's chosen are held in such slight esteem reflects the same cynicism about human motives which produced a constitutional structure of dispersed and fragmented authority. Designed more for safety than for speed or efficiency, America's governmental structure expresses a deep suspicion that the lust for power inheres in all mortals. The voters thus often trudge to the polls without enthusiasm, convinced that no man can withstand the temptations of office.

Nevertheless, since constitutions, written or unwritten, do not operate themselves, some credit for the longevity of

America's political system must go to those elected officials who have succeeded in reconciling the awesomely diverse and conflicting interests of a huge and restless nation. American politicians may be, as Lord Bryce remarked, of average intelligence and less than average virtue, but they have demonstrated a certain native genius for compromise that has kept the whole structure from tumbling down on their heads. Under the circumstances, one civil war in 200 years is not a bad record.

Geography itself places many demands on the political system. The continental United States stretches from the Atlantic to the Pacific across 3000 miles of forest, prairie, mountains and desert. The state of Alaska, detached to the north-west, spans roughly the same distance, and the island state of Hawaii lies about 2000 miles from the mainland. The great distances and variety of environments, ranging from arctic to tropical, assure wide differences in economic activities and in social attitudes. In the past, when the means of communication and transportation were feebler, sectional loyalties fiercely rivalled nationalistic sentiment; men were more likely to think of themselves as citizens of their home states than as citizens of the United States. Even today Americans tend to identify themselves with the interests of their regions, viewing national politics as a means of persuading Washington to do more for their regional agriculture or manufacturing. Rural denizens perceive their interests to be different from those of urban dwellers. Westerners suspiciously eye the 'Eastern establishment'; Southerners look warily upon the 'Yankees' to the north.

Besides geographical divisions, Americans are set apart from each other by distinct ethnic identities, which, while taking second place to national loyalty, are deeply held. Thus does the 'nation of immigrants' betray its origins. In the hundred years before 1921, when immigration was curtailed by federal law, America absorbed about 35 million foreigners, trusting in the assimilative powers of the schools and of the burgeoning economy. In this 'melting pot' the peoples of the world were to be 'Americanized', amalgamated into a new national alloy. But out of the crucible came an unexpected product. Professors Nathan Glazer and Daniel Moynihan have observed: 'As the groups were transformed by influences in American society, stripped of their original attributes, they were recreated as something new, but still as identifiable groups.' Politically these Irish-Americans, Italian-Americans and Polish-Americans behave as interest groups, measuring their power and well-being against that of others. In the large cities, where the 'ethnics' are concentrated, a political party usually finds it prudent to recognize this heterogeneity by running a 'balanced ticket': an Italian for mayor, a Pole for city council president, and an Irishman for comptroller.

The one ethnic group which has benefited least from assimilation is that which is marked off from the others by the colour of its skin. Imported as chattels since the early seventeenth century, blacks lost most of their African heritage and identity in the long night of slavery that ended with the Civil War of 1861–65. They received very little in return. The failure of the north to 'reconstruct' southern society and government after the war left the blacks to toil as sharecroppers (small tenant farmers) in the cotton and tobacco fields, a subsistence which recreated some of the worst features of medieval serfdom and none of the better ones. 'Jim Crow' laws excluded blacks from the franchise and segregated them from whites in schools, trains, shops and churches. The 'Second Reconstruction', the civil rights movement of the 1950s and 1960s, removed the shackles of legal segregation and gave southern blacks access to the ballot box. But the practical results so far have been relatively small. Blacks remain the poorest, worst-educated segment of the population. Having effected since the Second World War a mass migration to the northern and western cities, they remain largely isolated there in ghetto slums. In the south, the schools had been segregated by law, but in the north they were – and still are – segregated *de facto* by residential patterns enforced by white discrimination, a distinction which gives the blacks little solace.

Attempts to integrate the schools have provoked opposition just as intense as in the south. However, the blacks, who now compose about 15 per cent of the nation's population and a much larger proportion of the urban population, have at least begun to capture the reins of city government.

Against this background of sectional and ethnic loyalties, the politics of class plays a relatively small part. These attachments remain more salient than income level, even though the gap between upper and lower income groups in America is certainly not insubstantial and many obstacles encumber the ladder of social mobility. Class consciousness has not solidified in America, and socialist or workers' parties have never found a mass base. The integration of workers into democratic politics before industrialization created a true proletariat may help account for this attenuated sense of class. Property qualifications for voting disappeared early in the nineteenth century, while in Europe the working class typically had to force its way into the franchise by a collective effort.

A persuasive belief in economic opportunity and the absence of a distinctive working-class culture, furthermore, has sustained the notion that it is possible to become rich through hard work and luck. The lure of the 'big break', epitomized by the occasional celebrated success story, induces a man to rely more on his individual fortunes than on class solidarity to achieve material happiness. The general availability of higher education – since the establishment of state universities in the 1860s – has given some reality to this dream by affording relatively broad access to the better-paying occupations.

Moreover, Americans are comforted by the knowledge that to vault into the upper strata requires only money. There are no proper accents, only classless regional intonations, and one may become a thoroughly acceptable member of the elite by attending Texas Agricultural and Mechanical College as well as by attending Harvard – if one has a bank account to lend respectability. Even those who, in the despair of late middle age, abandon the hope of 'success' may confidently project their aspirations on to their progeny. As sociologists have discovered, most Americans, even quite poor ones, tend to identify themselves as 'middle class' or at worst 'lower middle class', convinced that they hover on the brink of being 'comfortably off'. There is, really, no alternative to this striving for material success; it is the only socially acceptable thing to do. One cannot take shelter in being a staunch member of a working class which does not believe it exists.

The trade union movement, therefore, plays a tactical rather than a strategic game. Although American trade unions are often described as 'non-political', that is true only in the sense that they, unlike European unions, make no pretence of leading the workers towards socialism. Trade unions in America accept capitalistic free enterprise, upon whose continued robust health their bounteous wages depend. The unions do, however, participate avidly in electoral politics and lobbying, considering themselves interest groups not very different from those of businessmen. Their object is to win by legislation practical benefits for the 25 per cent of the workforce that is 'organized'. Samuel Gompers, a founder of the American labour movement, summed up the ideology of the trade unions in three words: 'More and more.' Politics is a way to get more, such as minimum wage laws, social security pensions and unemployment benefits. For the unions, in fact, political power preceded and made possible economic power – the reverse of the European experience. It was federal legislation of the 1930s which secured for unions the legal right to employer recognition and collective bargaining, a position of strength that they were unable to win by industrial action alone.

Underlying all of this, of course, is that Americans are, in historian David Potter's phrase, a 'people of plenty'. The abundance of the American continent, as exploited by technology, furnished even the bottom of society a standard of living undreamed of in many other countries, and the continuing dynamism of the economy made opportunity for all more than a remote aspiration. Working-class ideology in Europe always assumed that equality necessarily entailed expropriating wealth from the rich and distributing it among the poor. The pie was fixed, and the only issue was how big a slice each segment of society would get. Naturally, the upper and lower strata retreated behind formidable barricades of class ideology to protect their claims to the national wealth. But America has always relied upon its power to generate more wealth to ameliorate incipient social discontent; no one need quibble about the just size of his slice because the pie could always be enlarged. The poor might achieve material well-being by sharing in new wealth rather than by taking the portion of the rich. Equality of result would not be assured, but that was not important so long as there was equality of opportunity. Even the unrich would still be well-off, by world standards, with their modest share of the national wealth.

Symbolic of the cornucopia was the nineteenth-century western frontier. While land was a fixed and scarce resource in Europe, in America it was for a long time virtually free to anyone with the fortitude to claim and work it. During most of the twentieth century there has been an expanding industrial economy and rising level of real income. Poverty became the predicament of a minority, rather than the fate of the majority. By the 1960s the government could aspire to relieve even that minority, by waging a 'war on poverty' that would eradicate material deprivation as if it were the vestige of a formerly dread epidemic disease.

Freed from the divisive pressure of scarcity, America does not have a left and a right confronting each other with totally incompatible notions of the good, the true and the beautiful. All have in common the value of maximizing their own share of the wealth, and they see in politics merely a mechanism for distributing it. Politics is thus sometimes described as about 'who get what, when and how'.

The modern prospect of chronic energy and resource shortage – of reduced economic growth, that is – raises the question of whether the American system would work very well without abundance. The necessity for prolonged rationing, conservation and austerity could impose strains with which the usual politics cannot cope. A system whose legitimacy depends on its continuing ability to give access to wealth may lack the power to authoritatively parcel out the meagre portions necessitated by scarcity.

So far American politics has been a struggle not between left and right but among myriad organized interest groups competing for an even larger share of the rewards which government can confer. Some of these rewards are purely financial: subsidies, tax credits, contracts, jobs, public works projects, insurance schemes and social benefits. Any given taxpayer is likely to measure his political 'clout' by whether he gets more out of government than he puts into it. Other rewards may be indirectly financial, such as legislation and regulations allowing one's private economic interests to thrive. A third type of reward is government legislation that makes the world the kind one likes to live in: those who favour legalized gambling or an end to capital punishment, for example, will try to translate their personal values into government policy.

In popular American political thought, as in the theory of free enterprise, the concept of the 'public good' is undefinable *a priori*; it is simply the net outcome of all the pushing and shoving among interest groups. The invisible hand of providence guides the nation's policy much as it determines the price of potatoes in the open market. Each group, of course, strives to identify its private good with the nebulous public good as a tactic; in that context, it seems not so egregious for the president of a car company to proclaim: 'What's good for General Motors is good for the country.'

The interaction among competitive groups is commonly referred to as 'pluralism'. To many political scientists pluralism is the essence of American democracy, much as it smacks of greed and self-interest. They consider it a healthy phenomenon, assuming that the groups are vigorously competitive and balance each other. Pluralism implies that decisions are founded upon compromise and that various facets of society have a voice in government. Policy automatically represents a consensus. Each group goes away with the satisfying feeling that it has got whatever was possible. No group is completely dominant, and none is shut out and left to smoulder with resentment. The upshot of pluralism, therefore, is contentment and stability. The evils of 'faction', so feared by the nation's founding fathers, are done away with, not by abolishing factions but by rejoicing in their multiplicity and their natural tendency to hold each other in check.

There is, however, another school of political science which doubts that reality conforms to this sanguine theoretical model. While not denying that many groups contend for power, the school of 'elite theorists' argues that not all groups are equal. Some groups are more powerful and more consistently successful than others. The successful groups monopolize the channels of access to government decision-makers, who tend to regard them as the embodiment of the general will. Moreover, argue the elite theorists, many interests in society are not represented by an organized group, and so their claims are never on the bargaining table. Facing no countervailing force, or no effective force, the small number of officially recognized interest groups constitute, in effect, governing elites.

The elite theorists offer a critique that must seriously qualify the optimistic model of the pluralists. It is easy to see, for example, that while well-paid lobby agents fight bravely in Washington on behalf of the National Association of Manufacturers, the consumers of the manufactured products are not similarly deployed as a compact phalanx. And while the American Federation of Labor-Congress of Industrial Organizations speaks with authority for organized labour, the majority of labourers are not heard at all. However, it must be conceded that at least the possibility of organizing the unorganized into a potent interest group always remains open. Consumers, for one, are beginning to make their presence felt through political action groups. What lies behind any interest group is the voting power and the combined financial resources of its members. When public policy affects a large number of persons, or even a modest number concentrated in a few constituencies, they are in a position to flex their muscles.

But that merely shades the basic picture of American politics as a huge distribution network, a kind of Arabian souk whose alleys are thronged with purveyors and purchasers haggling over the terms of sale. As such, the participants are not usually described in terms of 'left' and 'right' but in terms of a continuum from 'liberal' to 'conservative'. They all fundamentally agree that government should be employed in a positive fashion to achieve some goals; what really divides them is the question of what the goals are, or rather how much the government should do and for whom. Conservatives claim to oppose 'Big Government', both as a dispenser of funds and promulgator of regulations. But what they are really opposed to is particular kinds of government activity, chiefly welfare state expenditures and restrictions upon private enterprise. They do not object when government subsidizes business, as it does the merchant marine and the airlines, for example, or uses its regulatory power to protect private oligopolies from the perils of free competition, as it does in the case of the railroads. What conservatives desire, in essence, is government policies which heed the maxim that 'the business of America is business'.

While conservatives tend to equate every new welfare programme with squadrons of officious, bumbling bureaucrats, liberals are more confident of the creative power of administration to alleviate social and economic distress. The war on poverty of the 1960s exemplified the liberal faith that any evil could be obliterated by bombarding it with salvoes of money aimed by benign officials.

Periodic economic recessions illuminate the difference between liberals and conservatives. Both accept the need for government stimulation of the economy. The liberals advocate direct government intervention by creating public jobs and extending unemployment insurance. The conservatives prefer an indirect stimulus: tax credits and other incentives to private business expansion.

Different parts of the panoply of rights guaranteed by the

constitution against abridgement by government are held most sacred by conservatives and liberals. To the conservative, the right to property is all important. Liberals consider property less holy than the non-economic rights enshrined in the constitution, such as freedom of speech and religion; government may curtail economic liberty but no other.

That is the domestic affairs component of liberalism and conservatism, but the two positions are also distinguished by different attitudes towards foreign relations. Since the Second World War, at least, conservatives have espoused the 'hard line'. They have been the Cold Warriors *par excellence*, advocating a powerful military presence abroad and support of any 'Free World' dictator who seemed able to withstand communism, regardless of how little freedom he allowed his subjects. Liberals, on the other hand, particularly since the 1960s, have argued for a policy of negotiation and compromise with the Eastern bloc, an easing of the arms race, and the promotion of mutual ties through trade and scientific exchange. In finding allies abroad, the liberals have contended, the United States should build defences against communism by reinforcing democratic processes in other countries, rather than by undermining them in favour of a strong-man. Having said that, one must take notice of the fact that American leaders tend to shift their international outlooks rather easily. The most outstanding example of this in recent memory was the transformation of Richard M. Nixon from arch-foe of the communist menace to engineer of *détente* with China and the Soviet Union. Nixon was able to persuade other conservatives to his point of view by making them realize that 'trading with the enemy' could be sound business as well as sound diplomacy.

Changing one's political complexion is made easier by the fact that the conservative–liberal distinction does not coincide with party lines. The Democratic ranks are heavy with liberals, the Republican ranks with conservatives. Each party, nevertheless, harbours an important minority of the opposite persuasion. Many Democrats, including those who have held powerful posts in Congress, are as conservative as a conservative Republican, and some Republicans are as liberal as a liberal Democrat. This intra-party heterodoxy, to some extent, resulted from historical accidents which have hardened into traditional partisan loyalties. The staunch conservative contingent in the Democratic party, for example, consists primarily of southerners, because Republicans were virtually routed from state politics in the south after the Civil War. A Republican administration had prosecuted the war for the north, and Republican congressmen were held responsible for the much resented post-war Reconstruction laws. Now that these bitter memories have begun to fade in the south, the Republican party is starting to re-establish an effective two-party system there, but whether southern conservatism will fully convert to Republicanism, thereby placing most conservatives in one camp and permitting the parties to re-align along doctrinal lines, remains doubtful.

American parties would seem destined, by their very structure, never to have much uniformity of political persuasion. At the national level, at least, each party is something of a front organization for a mosaic of autonomous state parties which share not much more than the use of the party label at election times. The names Republican and Democrat thus mean different things in different places. Conservative sections of the country elect conservative Democrats and conservative Republicans; liberal areas produce liberal Democrats and liberal Republicans.

One consequence of this is the weakness of party discipline in Congress. When the senators and representatives assemble in Congress, they organize themselves formally along party lines, but the voting, often as not, conforms more closely to the conservative–liberal division than to party affiliation. Virtually every bill requires a coalition of Republicans and Democrats in order to pass. Such an arrangement may seem impossibly confusing compared to that of the British Parliament, where two parties committed to opposing principles face each other across an abyss. A member of the Tory left might share some views with a right-wing Labourite, but he would not be expected to have much in common with a left-wing Labourite. Yet congressmen accept implicitly the notion that the conservative and liberal wings of each party are quite similar, because each party spans the broad spectrum of opinion.

Parties exist, one might almost say, to satisfy the need for an organizing principle in the legislatures and a mechanism for nominating two candidates for elective office. A man of any persuasion might flip a coin to choose his party, and indeed, some interest groups do flit back and forth between parties to maximize their leverage. The Tweedledum and Tweedledee of Republican and Democrat emphasizes the degree of consensus on fundamental issues and the extent to which politics is simply a struggle over the distribution of the booty.

By focusing on distribution, rather than on partisan ideology, the party system properly addresses itself to the crucial issue. For although the nation is constitutionally dedicated to political and legal equality, it is not similarly dedicated to economic equality. Indeed, it is committed to an economic system which maximizes efficiency of production at the expense of equal distribution of the product. Yet there is no doubt that political equality can seem an empty shell in the presence of gross economic inequality. Under modern conditions and expectations, political equality is simply not very satisfying without a commensurate standard of living. Moreover, it is myopic to deny that the possession of disproportionately large economic resources can be translated into disproportionately large political privileges, for, as the economist Arthur M. Okun has said, 'dollars transgress on rights'. The law indeed forbids both the rich and poor alike from sleeping under bridges. That being so, the function of democratic politics is to relieve the tension between constitutional principles and economic principles. By redistributing part of the natural production, it makes economic reality correspond somewhat more closely to constitutional theory.

2 The Constitution: On Paper and In Practice

To unite thirteen sparsely settled agricultural colonies into a single commonwealth is one thing; to govern a populous, industrialized nation spanning a continent is quite another. The marvel of the United States Constitution is that it has done both. Of course, the constitution is not precisely the same document that it was originally; it has been formally amended twenty-six times, and numerous informal institutions and conventions have supplemented the actual text. But on the whole, the system still functions according to the plan laid down in the eighteenth century.

Whether that is something to be admired or regretted depends upon one's point of view. Foreign observers often portray America as thrashing about inside an eighteenth-century straitjacket, hardly able to contain the robust spirit of the modern age. Americans, on the other hand, look upon the constitution with an uncritical acceptance which may be due more to gratitude for faithful service than to any rational calculation of present or future usefulness.

No doubt the constitution has stultified the national attitude towards government. American political philosophy begins and ends with exegesis of the holy writ, paying more attention to what the framers intended in 1787 than to what the citizens who live under that document today might wish. But Americans surely may be forgiven for treating the constitution as a totemic object, since they seek in it answers not so much about the mechanisms of government as about the spirit that lies behind their government. Principles have been the constitution's chief blessing to the American people, because they are principles which have commanded and continue to command universal allegiance. No ideology, no ethnic or geographical division, no economic conflict of interest has destroyed the consensus on principles which the constitution embodies. In that sense, the constitution is no more an irrelevant relic of eighteenth-century America than the Bible is of ancient Palestine.

That the constitution lays down general principles of governmental structure and operation, rather than minute details, is not the result of the framers' prescience but of their pragmatism. The constitution was created to cope with an immediate, pressing problem: were the thirteen colonies to be united under an effective, central government, or were they to go their own ways as separate sovereign nations? The constitution set about answering this limited question by proposing a general scheme of government. To have stipulated all details of the future government would have been imprudent; the framers hoped to win quick acceptance for the scheme as a whole, leaving the thornier problems for later. As Lord Bryce observed of the constitution a century after its drafting, it was a 'judicious mixture of definiteness in principle with elasticity of details'. Although acting from necessity, the framers' attention to the larger picture has given the constitution one of its enduring strengths. For the document was made more flexible than if it had specified the proper limits of governments as recognized in the eighteenth century. In later generations it would be possible, within the broad restrictions imposed, to operate a government that was effective by twentieth-century standards.

Even if the framers wished to go into more detail, there would have been no occasion for it. The new nation was formed by assembling building blocks, the states, whose existence had to be accepted as a *fait accompli*. Since the states would continue to exercise many powers, it was not necessary to prescribe in the federal constitution every governmental function down to the pettiest detail of local administration. Given the exigencies of the day, there was no chance of the framers losing sight of the main goal.

When the constitution was first conceived, it was not at all clear to most American colonists that they needed anything more than a few amendments to the Articles of Confederation, which loosely bound the colonies in a kind of league following the War of Independence. The league, it was true, had manifested troubling defects; trade between the states was burdened by currency and tariff problems, the national legislature found itself unable to effectively levy taxes, and the states were reluctant to contribute troops to the national defence force. Yet many colonists wondered if they were destined to be a single nation. Could such imposing geographical distances be mastered, such differences in economic activity be overcome? Having just tossed the yoke of imperium from their necks, would the states voluntarily submit to another large central government whose benign or malignant intentions they could not securely predict?

If there were any doubts, they were settled by the ominous presence throughout the hemisphere of foreign powers – Britain, France, and Spain – who, it was feared, would make short work of the divided colonies. The problem thus presented was to devise a scheme of government which would create a unified, militarily strong nation while, at the same time, preserving the liberties that had been so dearly and so recently won. There would be other compromises as well, as the drafting proceeded, reconciling competing geographical and economic interests, but the overriding concern in the minds of the framers was for balancing liberty with order – or, looked at another way, for creating just enough government.

That the colonists perceived the problem of government as a tension between liberty and order has been attributed to the influence of John Locke. Certainly, the Declaration of Independence in 1776 had spoken as if a social compact between the colonial subjects and the British monarch existed, and it echoed Locke's belief that the natural rights of man limited the purposes for which the state is formed. 'The community,' he had argued, 'perpetually retains a supreme power of saving themselves from the attempts and designs of anybody, even their legislators, whenever they shall be so foolish or so wicked as to lay and carry on designs against the liberties and properties of the subject.' Similar sentiments resonate through the Declaration:

> We hold these truths to be self-evident, that all men are created equal, that they are endowed by their Creator with certain inalienable Rights, that among these are Life, Liberty and the pursuit of Happiness. That to secure these rights, Governments are instituted among Men, deriving their just powers from the consent of the governed. That whenever any Form of Government becomes destructive of these ends, it is the Right of the People to alter or abolish it . . .

Yet one should not credit unduly the influence of philosophers where the first-hand experience of tyrannical government had been so distinctly unpleasant. Determined to profit from the bitter memories of crown rule, the framers knew at least what they did not want the new government to be.

In their minds, the basic lesson was that individual liberties are fragile when government is absolute. They did not reject the British form of government outright; they merely found it flawed in practice by the excessive power of the executive. They were impressed by Montesquieu's argument, that England enjoyed relatively great liberty because the functions of government were distributed among executive, legislative and judicial organs, each balancing the other's cravings for absolute power. That made sense to the framers because of their knowledge of events in England, and because of the political history of the American colonies, where the elected legislature often posed the only counterweight to a crown-appointed governor. As one of the framers, James Madison, remarked, 'the accumulation of all powers, legislative, executive, and judiciary, in the same hands . . . may justly be pronounced the very definition of tyranny.'

The framers were also firmly convinced of the value of the English common law in protecting the liberties of subjects. The common law showed how limits might be placed upon arbitrary governmental actions. No one could be subjected by the state to penalties unless found guilty of previously specified offences, according to an established procedure. Limiting offences to those enunciated in the laws and binding judicial procedure by fixed rules precluded the capricious exercise of authority. Moreover, the colonists had been able to observe the common law in action; religious and political dissenters had often been saved from persecution by a sympathetic jury. The features of common law criminal prosecutions would thus be very closely copied in the Bill of Rights that was added to the constitution, but even more important than the specific mechanisms of indictment and jury trial was the underlying assumption: that law could limit even the sovereign.

The founder's faith in the power of the rule of law to check arbitrary, hence despotic, government, led them to write a document, a fundamental law, that would govern the rulers as well as the ruled. England almost alone among monarchies rejected the principle that the 'king can do no wrong', and in that notion of a 'higher law', binding even monarchs, lay the origin of the American's belief in the constitution as a guarantee of liberty.

The common law also afforded a seminal example for the framers in that it was not chiefly statute law, the commands of a sovereign, but rather emanated from the people, from their customs as 'found' and declared by the judges. Unlike statute law, which the sovereign gives and just as easily takes, the common law was deeply rooted in usage. It was a permanent fixture of national life. Although constantly evolving, it could no more be abolished at a stroke than the people could be abruptly wrenched from their daily habits by governmental fiat. The founders esteemed the common law even more because of a misapprehension that its principles, as then known, dated from time immemorial. As Professor Edwin S. Corwin has observed: 'The idea was, obviously, a politically valuable one, since it proclaimed from the first the existence of a body of law owing nothing to royal authority and capable therefore of setting limits to that authority.'

The constitution would assume that same aura of imperviousness to the whim of authority. In a single act of legislation, the people enacted a fundamental law. Their elected representatives could then legislate within those broad boundaries but could not change them. The people remained sovereign, not the government. That largely accounts for the reverence in which the constitution is held, for it is not only a blueprint for a system of government, it is also the authentic voice of a sovereign people.

Although the founding fathers, as their title would imply, are generally remembered as heroic law-givers, a revisionist school of historians argues that love of liberty was, at the very least, not the sole motive of those who drafted the constitution. In the document's carefully constructed safeguards against simple majority rule and in the various protections for private property the revisionists see the conspiracy of a wealthy elite. Attempts by state legislatures to tamper with the sanctity of property and the rights of creditors had left men of property feeling threatened by unbridled democracy, the revisionists contend, and convinced them of the need for a national government, not easily susceptible to majority control, which would repress the expropriative urges of the states.

The controversy between revisionist and traditional interpretations is not likely to be resolved conclusively. The constitutional convention delegates were, to be sure, members of the upper classes in their respective states, and they evidenced in the debates an unabashed desire for a document that would afford protection for property. One of the Virginia delegates termed it the 'principal object of government'. Political support for the document once drafted, moreover, was strongest in the cities and the coastal areas, the stronghold of the commercial interests, while opposition was stoutest among the small farmers of the interior. On the other hand, few men were unpropertied, since land was plentiful, so that the security of private property was a general concern. Although the electorate in all states at that time had to meet a property requirement for voting, most adult males were eligible for the franchise. It was these voters, in fact, who elected delegates to the state conventions that ultimately ratified the constitution. Many of the leading opponents of ratification, moreover, were drawn from the same class as those who drafted the document.

Conflicts between large and small property-owners, or between agrarian and commercial interests, there may have been, but these would hardly support a conspiracy theory because other, cross-cutting interests also influenced popular attitudes toward the new constitution. The large states, for example, favoured representation in Congress according to population, while the small states favoured equal representation, regardless of population. The framers compromised by providing equal representation in the Senate and representation according to population in the House. Another compromise resolved a sectional argument between north and south over the slave population: three fifths of the slaves would be counted both for determining representation in Congress and for levying *per capita* taxes.

Whether it was the result of a conspiracy or a national consensus, the constitution did provide a notably salubrious environment for commercial enterprise. The federal government was given supervision of interstate and foreign commerce, thus removing the state boundaries as barriers to trade and cementing together a national marketplace. The government was also empowered to establish uniform bankruptcy laws, coin money, standardize weights and measures, and secure patent rights to individuals. The states were prohibited from interfering with the 'obligation of contract'. The debts of the states were assumed by the federal government, assuring that bond holders would not lose their investments. Direct taxation of individuals by the federal government was limited to *per capita* assessments, thereby excluding the possibility of a graduated income tax that would impinge more heavily upon the wealthy. Finally, the Fifth Amendment, adopted shortly after ratification, assured that 'No person shall be . . . deprived of life, liberty or property, without due process of law; nor shall private property be taken for public use without just compensation.' Taken together, these provisions would seem to create the ideal Lockeian order, a government dedicated to promoting individual acquisitiveness. Whether this order was founded upon philosophic conviction or sheer cupidity is probably beyond our knowing; the two are often conjoined.

The constitution was wrought in the name of 'We, the people', by delegates from the states who met in Philadelphia during the summer of 1787. The constitutional convention had been called in desperation after a meeting to try to mend the defects of the Articles of Confederation concluded that the old order was beyond repair. Although the delegates at Philadelphia debated at length, they drafted a document which is, among constitutions at least, remarkably succinct.

In a total of approximately 7000 words, the document sets out the structure of government, enumerates the powers of each branch and divides the functions of the federal government from those of the state governments. It is much shorter than most national constitutions (and American state constitutions) and presents a curious mixture of sweeping generality and painstaking attention to some details that the modern reader may not think terribly important. Why, one wonders, would the framers bother to specify that trials for treason must be based on the evidence of at least two witnesses, while forgetting to include something as important as whether a state has a right to secede from the union? Fortunately for the future United States, the constitution usually managed to be vague in the right places, leaving some play in the joints for later interpreters.

The framers' attachment to separation of powers is plain from the organization of the articles. Article I vests the legislative powers in the Senate and House of Representatives, Article II places the executive power in the hands of the President, and Article III confers the judicial power upon one Supreme Court and such inferior courts as Congress may wish to establish. Article IV discusses the relationship that shall exist among the states and between the states and the federal government; Article V prescribes methods for amending the constitution; Article VI is a miscellaneous section, whose most important provision declares that the constitution and federal laws made under it take precedence over all state enactments. Article VII announces that the constitution will take effect when nine of the thirteen states ratify it.

The basic plan is diffusion or fragmentation of power. The lines of division run both horizontally, between the federal government and the states, and vertically, between the three branches of the federal government. The legislative branch itself is subdivided into two co-equal houses. In separating powers among the executive, legislative and judicial branches, however, the framers did not assign each a totally distinct function; rather they made each share the function of government in such a manner as to be dependent on the other. The system of 'checks and balances' thus relies not upon independence but inter-dependence among the branches. Congress would enact legislation, but the President could veto it. The courts would construe the law, but the judges would be appointed by the President with the consent of the Senate.

The framers' suspicions, however, did not end there. What would happen if all three branches were somehow in collusion? To preclude that eventuality, the framers took pains to make each component of the government dependent upon a different 'constituency', a different base of support. The plan, in Madison's words, was to give each 'the necessary constitutional means and personal motives to resist encroachment on the others . . . Ambition must be made to counteract ambition.' Thus, the Senate was to be elected by the state legislatures, the members of the House by small popular constituencies, and the President by electors selected by each state in whatever way it wished.

The terms of officials, moreover, were made to vary – two years for the House, six for the Senate, four for the Presidency – and to overlap so that no sudden popular majority would be able to seize control of the entire government. Such a majority might sweep up most of the House seats in an election but still find the President with two years remaining in his term. Should the majority work its will in a Presidential election, it would still find two thirds of the Senate firmly in place. The judges were secured in their independence by lifetime tenure.

The plan, in brief, was to make it impossible for the government to act unless all the branches of government, representing varied constituencies and chosen at different times, were in agreement. However much that arrangement might seem like a guarantee of governmental inertia, a built-in proclivity for doing nothing, such, in the framers' minds, was the price of avoiding tyranny. This form of government has never laid claim to decisiveness, but it has on the whole accomplished what it was intended to do: prevent the accumulation of unchecked power. No institution in the American government enjoys complete control over anything. In Britain, the cabinet, sitting as a committee of the majority in Parliament, exercises the full authority of government, but no comparable locus of power exists in America.

The constitution, of course, confers great powers upon the national government, as well as imposing heavy impediments. More than half the text is devoted to the first article, outlining the powers of Congress and, by inference, the scope of the federal government. The key provision is section 8 of the article, which gives Congress authority to levy taxes, issue currency, establish post offices, create courts, declare war, provide a defence force and regulate commerce among the states and with foreign nations. These 'enumerated powers' appear to represent the minimum authority that must be possessed by any government and surely must be capable of being expanded to meet changing conditions. But the tradition of constitutional interpretation has wavered uncertainly between the poles of 'loose construction' and 'strict construction'.

The loose constructionists have been mindful of Chief Justice John Marshall's admonition in the early nineteenth century that 'we must never forget that it is *a constitution* we are expounding', a broad enabling charter intended to create a competent government, not a paraplegic among nations.

Such a constitution could not have authorized President Jefferson, in so many words, to purchase the Louisiana Territory from France in 1806, because no one could have guessed that it would be offered for sale. Yet to forego the opportunity to acquire the entire Mississippi River basin would have been foolhardy. The strict constructionists, however, contended then, as they do now, that the constitution says precisely what it means and nothing more; to depart from its literal meaning, no matter how worthy the object, is to abandon the original scheme of limited government.

Fortunately for the loose constructionists, the last paragraph of section 8 authorized Congress 'to make all laws which shall be necessary and proper for carrying into execution the foregoing powers'. Never has so much been said in so few words. For this so-called 'elastic clause' suggested that while Congress could address itself only to the *ends* that were enumerated, it had a relatively free choice of *means*.

The pattern for expansive interpretation of the implied powers in the elastic clause was set by Marshall in the classic case of *McCulloch v. Maryland* in 1819. Faced with the question of whether the United States could establish a national bank, Marshall wrote: 'Let the end be legitimate, let it be within the scope of the Constitution, and all means which are appropriate, which are plainly adapted to that end, which are not prohibited . . . are constitutional.' To adapt to new conditions, later interpreters have gladly heeded Marshall's dictum. Thus, although the constitution is naturally silent on whether Congress can appropriate funds to send men to the moon, it can be argued that the space programme is a means towards the end of providing for the common defence. The alleged connection between means and ends may be even more tenuous than that. Congress, for example, financed the building of a network of interstate motorways under the pretext that they were national defence highways, even though it was unlikely that they would be needed to rush tanks to the Canadian or Mexican borders to repel invasions.

No provision of the constitution has been a more fertile

source of implied powers than the 'commerce clause', because the regulation of trade naturally encompasses myriad activities. Significantly, the constitution did not say *why* commerce should be regulated or for what purpose. Congress was not charged with promoting capitalism or socialism, improving the lot of workers, removing health hazards or keeping stock prices bullish. From that we may infer that the framers simply desired orderly trade, under a single set of rules, regardless of what the rules were, since uncertainty is the *bête noire* of the businessmen. Indeed, the profusion of state commercial codes, tariffs and currencies that had so impeded interstate trade was a primary motive for federating.

Because the commerce clause fails to specify the goals of regulation, Congress is free to exercise that power to accomplish purposes which are only peripherally economic. It is not limited to providing an arena for orderly competition, standardizing weights and measures and smoothing out the bumps in the business cycle. Virtually any evil – child labour, racial discrimination or car exhaust fumes – may be declared inimical to interstate commerce and restricted or banned. When Congress, in the Civil Rights Act of 1964, outlawed racial discrimination in hotels and restaurants, it found its authority in the commerce power; Congress could compel service to blacks in the remotest snack bar because the hamburgers had been shipped in interstate commerce. The real objection to racism was not that it burdened commerce, but commerce furnished the pretext for remedying a social injustice.

During the early decades of the republic, the struggle of the federal government to assert its hegemony over the states took the form of a battle over the extent of the commerce power. Jealous of their privileges, the states exploited the failure of the constitution to specify just where intrastate trade ended and interstate trade began. The problem persisted well into the twentieth century, seriously hampering the federal government in its effort to regulate large-scale corporate capitalism. In the eighteenth century most enterprises existed wholly within a state, subject to its laws, and only the movement of goods across state lines fell under federal control. But when corporations in the late nineteenth century began establishing branches and plants in several states, it became an arguable point whether they came under state or federal jurisdiction. It was clear, however, that the unco-ordinated attempts of a number of states to regulate corporations would prove ineffectual. Not until the 1930s did the Supreme Court adopt a broad concept of interstate commerce that freed the government to deal with the social and economic problems of industrialization and corporate capitalism. Today the commerce clause is the textual basis for the government's inescapable responsibility to manage the economy on a grand scale.

The growth of the commerce power through judicial interpretation exemplifies one important method of adapting the constitution to constantly changing conditions. It is probably a more useful, if less forthright, method than formal amendment because judicial interpretation is a continuous and incremental process, whereas amending is cumbersome, time-consuming and intermittent. Before the process of ratification is complete, a proposed amendment may seem like an idea whose time has come and gone. But the amending process, although sparingly used, remains an important piece of auxiliary equipment for modernizing the constitution when there is a clear consensus that change is necessary. The amendment provision was to the framers a built-in self-renewal mechanism, enabling the nation to perfect its institutions in the light of experience. Madison thought the amendment process a nice balance between precipitate change and petrification of political institutions. 'It guards equally,' he wrote, 'against that extreme facility, which would render the Constitution too mutable; and that extreme difficulty, which might perpetuate its discovered faults.'

The constitution prescribes two methods for proposing amendments, one giving the initiative to the states, another to the federal government. Under the former method, the legislature of two thirds of the states may request Congress to call a convention for the purpose of drafting amendments. That method has never been used because of uncertainty about the procedures that such a convention would follow. There is also a lurking danger that once convened, the delegates might decide, like the founding fathers, to propose an entirely new constitution. Whether Congress could limit the scope of the convention is unclear. For these reasons, the much simpler alternative method of proposing amendments by a two thirds vote of both houses of Congress has invariably been employed.

Amendments proposed by either route become part of the constitution when ratified by the legislatures of three quarters (38) of the states, or if Congress chooses, by convention in three quarters of the states. The convention method has been used only once, to prevent the representatives of 'dry' rural areas, who dominated the state legislatures, from defeating the Twenty-first Amendment, repealing prohibition of alcoholic beverages. Usually, Congress will set a deadline of seven years for accumulating the requisite number of state ratifications, thus precluding the possibility that a long-dormant proposal might suddenly be approved decades after it had been forgotten about.

The amending process has been used only sporadically. The first ten amendments were adopted in 1791, shortly after the constitution was ratified, in order to satisfy the demand for a bill of rights. Two amendments were added by 1804, but none during the next sixty-one years. Between 1865 and 1870, after the Civil War, the three 'Reconstruction Amendments' were passed, ending slavery, enfranchising the blacks, and guaranteeing citizens of all colours 'equal protection of the laws'. There was then a hiatus until 1913, when the rising political philosophy of Progressivism brought about the enactment of the Sixteenth Amendment, providing for the federal income tax, and the Seventeenth, which called for senators to be popularly elected rather than chosen by the state legislatures.

In 1919, a campaign by the temperance movement culminated in ratification of the Eighteenth or 'Prohibition

Amendment', which outlawed 'intoxicating liquors'. The Suffragette Movement provided the impetus for adopting the Nineteenth Amendment, in 1920, granting the vote to women. The Twentieth Amendment, ratified in 1933, abolished the 'lame duck' session of Congress, between December and March, during which congressmen defeated in the November elections could continue to influence legislation. The same year the Twenty-first Amendment ended the prohibition (and bootlegging) era by repealing the Eighteenth Amendment.

Franklin D. Roosevelt's four terms as President raised fears of elective dictatorship that led to the passage of the Twenty-second Amendment (1951), limiting chief executives to two terms, the customary limit adhered to by Roosevelt's predecessors. By the Twenty-third Amendment (1961), the residents of Washington were given the right to vote in presidential elections; because the capital is technically the 'District of Columbia', administered directly by Congress, its residents had been denied the franchise. Among the first fruits of the civil rights movement was the Twenty-fourth Amendment (1964), which prohibited imposition of a poll tax as a prerequisite for voting in federal elections. Southern states traditionally had employed a poll tax as a device for discouraging black voters.

The Twenty-fifth Amendment (1967) was prompted by the desire to assure a stable line of succession to the Presidency. It provides that when a Vice President succeeds a President, the Vice Presidency shall be filled by a nominee of the new President, confirmed by a majority of both houses of Congress. The ,amendment also sets out a procedure for temporary succession by the Vice President in case of presidential disability.

The Twenty-sixth Amendment (1971) established the voting age for all federal and state elections at eighteen years; in most states, the voting age had been twenty-one even though young persons were becoming politically aware at a much earlier age – and went to war at eighteen.

In 1972 Congress proposed a Twenty-seventh Amendment, dubbed the Equal Rights Amendment, which would prohibit the 'equality of rights under law' from being denied on account of one's sex. An upshot of the feminist movement, the amendment would buttress the 'equal protection' clause of the Fourteenth Amendment.

The amending process, obviously, has helped to keep the constitution responsive to contemporary sensibilities. The table of amendments is a geological record of the political movements which have swept the nation. An amendment usually marks the culmination of a movement, the time when its once radical ideas have achieved respectability. That so few amendments in all have been adopted – most state constitutions have had many more in a shorter period – and that only one has been repealed testifies to the correctness of Madison's belief that the amendment process would achieve a balance between too much and too little change.

The conservative forces in society have been conspicuously less successful in the politics of the amending process than the liberals. Prohibition proved to be a short-lived victory; the two-term Presidency, if seen as a reaction to Rooseveltian democracy, is perhaps its only signal achievement in modern times. Many are the proposed conservative amendments, on the other hand, which have fallen by the wayside. Conservatives have pressed for amendments to restrict the treaty-making powers of the federal government and to limit the level of income taxation. Several liberal decisions of the Supreme Court provoked proposals to restrict court-ordered reapportionment of the state legislatures, to allow Bible-reading in the public schools, and to prohibit bussing of students to achieve school integration. In each of these instances, recourse to the amending process was a last-ditch attempt to thwart changes which the conservatives had been unable to prevent by ordinary political means.

In addition to judicial interpretation and formal amendments, custom and usage help ensure the flexibility of the constitution. Beside the written constitution has grown up a kind of unwritten constitution, a collection of institutions which have been sanctioned by time and accorded universal acceptance. Among these customary adaptations is the cabinet. Although the constitution merely refers to a 'principal officer in each of the executive departments', Presidents have always treated these officers collectively as a cabinet, albeit lacking all the features of a cabinet responsible to a legislature. The system of standing committees in Congress likewise carries no constitutional authorization but has become firmly embedded in the institutional structure.

The most astonishing of all the extra-constitutional adaptations, considering the attitudes of the framers, has been the development of political parties. The constitution does not mention parties, and we know from their fulminations against the spirit of 'faction' that the founding fathers hoped parties would not develop. Indeed, the fragmentation of political power among the branches and between the federal and state levels was intended to prevent any one party from governing. Yet parties quickly made their appearance after the constitution was ratified and became a significant feature of the political system. 'Would they [the framers] be shocked or merely surprised,' Professor Clinton Rossiter has aptly asked, 'to learn that one of the most effective checks in our enduring system of checks and balances is the party in opposition . . .?'

3 Federalism and its Discontents

When they met in 1787, the framers knew of only two possible models for the new commonwealth: a national government, whose writ ran everywhere, or a confederation of sovereign states. It was their happy fortune to discover, by a compromise between the proponents of each, a third system, blending elements of national and confederal government. Federalism, American style, was to mean a national authority, supreme within the sphere assigned to it, and a number of states continuing to exercise sovereign prerogatives within their own sphere.

Although it was a burning issue at the constitutional convention, the federal structure of the new government was outlined by the framers in a remarkably indirect, almost off-hand fashion. The constitution nowhere states plainly 'there shall be a federal form of government'. The words 'federal' or 'federalism' do not even appear in the text. The system must be deduced by reading between the lines. The constitution deals primarily with the powers and limitations of the central government. When the states are mentioned it is most often to prohibit them from a certain activity. Powers were delegated *from* the states, whose continued existence is taken for granted, *to* the central government. The states gained no authority from the constitution that they did not already enjoy, and they surrendered much.

Lest it be presumed that the states had given up too much, a terse qualifying statement was later appended as the Tenth Amendment: 'The powers not delegated to the United States by the Constitution, nor prohibited by it to the states, are reserved to the states respectively, or to the people.' This, the only general description of the role of the states, hardly says more than that, with the exceptions noted, the states are to carry on with whatever they had been doing. Nevertheless, the Tenth Amendment serves as the chapter and verse most often cited by 'states' rights' advocates, because it seems to confirm the states' traditional prerogatives and preclude their usurpation by the national government.

Since the states would not look kindly upon any plan which contemplated their extinction, some such arrangement was unavoidable. But the spectre of tyranny was also conducive to federalism. Although many in Philadelphia believed that a government holding sway over a vast territory was incompatible with republican liberty, they were persuaded ultimately that the chances of any single faction gaining total power diminished as the size and diversity of a nation increased. The opponents of centralized authority were reassured, furthermore, that the principle of balance of power would temper the relationship between the national and state governments.

But fear of centralization remains to this day. The threat of the national government overwhelming the states has been an enduring theme in American history. The dangers lurking in Washington have always been decried by champions of states' rights, who consider the erosion of state authority a threat to individual liberties. The states' rights position has attracted mainly those for whom the national government represents a threat to economic freedom or to such local customs as racial segregation. But the very persistence of the controversy reflects the steady growth in the power of national government during the last 200 years and the failure of the framers to define the federal relationship very precisely. The omission of any provision about secession of states from the union is particularly surprising. In later years, nationalists were to declare the union 'indestructible' and membership in it irreversible. If so, the framers were seriously derelict in forgetting to mention such an important abridgement of the states' sovereignty. Four years of civil war were required to finally extinguish the theoretical right to secede.

While the framers neglected to define their concept of the

federal union, some general principles stand out. The national government was obligated to guarantee the states a 'republican form of government' and to protect them from invasion and domestic violence. The constitution is also careful to assure the states a crucial role in the selection of members of the national legislature. The state legislatures were empowered to choose their senators, and the qualifications for voting for members of the House of Representatives were to be the same as those prescribed by each state legislature for elections to fill its lowest chamber. The 'times, places and manner' of holding elections were left to the states, subject to alteration by Congress. Thus, no congressional district crosses a state boundary, and the drawing of district lines – a crucial determinant in elections – is a valued privilege of the state legislatures.

A small but thorough catalogue of restrictions upon the states forms a codicil to the list of congressional powers in Article I. Among the proscribed activities are making treaties and alliances, coining money, granting titles of nobility, taxing imports and exports, and maintaining an army and navy in peacetime.

No state may enter into a compact with any other state without the consent of Congress. In practice, that has not been a barrier of much importance since the states have only rarely resorted to the device of compact to accomplish some mutual goal. Some states have entered into agreements to preserve natural resources, regulate common waterways or build bridges between their territories, but the preferred method of dealing with problems that overspill state boundaries is to entrust them to the central government.

The states are also enjoined to give 'full faith and credit' – that is, recognition – to each others' laws and judicial proceedings. While a state may only reluctantly accept 'quickie' divorces granted by Nevada, court orders entered in one jurisdiction are usually valid elsewhere. No state is required to enforce the criminal laws of another under the 'full faith and credit' clause, but a separate provision requires the return of fugitives from justice (and, formerly, runaway slaves). Most states have enacted uniform extradition laws, and Congress has made interstate flight to avoid prosecution a federal crime.

Each state, moreover, is required to grant persons from other states the same 'privileges and immunities' enjoyed by its own citizens. Non-residents may not be denied the right to engage in business, hold property and have access to the courts, nor may they be taxed in a discriminatory manner. However, the states have been allowed to treat them as a separate class for certain purposes; they may be charged higher tuition at the state university and prohibited from some state-licensed occupations, such as medicine. However, to become a full-fledged citizen of any state merely requires a brief period of residence. Restrictions on travel or emigration from one state to another have generally been held unconstitutional.

The capstone of the federal structure is the stern injunction in Article VI that the laws enacted by the national government 'shall be the supreme law of the land; and the judges in every state shall be bound thereby, anything in the constitution or laws of any state to the contrary notwithstanding.' In this, the 'supremacy clause', the framers served notice that when the national government acts within its sphere of competence, it sweeps incompatible state laws before it. At various times it has been contended that the states may 'nullify' the effect of federal legislation within their borders or 'interpose' their authority between their citizens and the enactments of the national government. The doctrines of nullification and interposition found particularly fruitful soil in the south, where they were espoused with great vigour in the period leading up to the Civil War. An echo of these doctrines was heard again in the 1950s and early 1960s when the national government forced racial integration upon southern schools.

But national supremacy has prevailed, in large measure because the Supreme Court, as umpire of conflicts between state and federal authority, has supported the supremacist position at crucial moments, particularly in the early decades of the republic. That the task of arbitrating such disputes should fall to the court was inevitable. The 'supremacy clause' addresses itself particularly to judges, and it soon became clear that the central government would founder if the Supreme Court could not restrain state judges from vitiating national legislation. The power of the Supreme Court to review state judicial decisions was firmly established by 1821, when Chief Justice Marshall, an ardent nationalist, averred in *Cohens v. Virginia* that nothing surrounding the framing of the constitution 'would justify the opinion that the confidence reposed in the states was so implicit as to leave in them and their tribunals the power of resisting or defeating, in the form of law, the legitimate measures of the union.' Marshall reminded the states that they were 'members of one great empire – for some purposes sovereign, for some purposes subordinate.'

The difficult question, however, was whether for any given purpose a state was sovereign or subordinate. The states and the national government shared many common purposes, exercising their powers concurrently. The national government levied taxes and regulated commerce, but so did the states. Each was within its proper sphere, yet the two levels of government might impinge upon each other. When Maryland had attempted to tax a branch of the Bank of the United States, Marshall declared that the states 'have no power, by taxation or otherwise, to retard, impede, burden, or in any manner control, the operations of the constitutional laws enacted by Congress.' The chief justice asserted that 'the government of the union, though limited in its powers, is supreme within its sphere of action'. And when New York State granted a private monopoly for steamship navigation on the Hudson River in 1808, the court invalidated it by announcing the principle that congressional power to regulate commerce takes precedence over any state enactment.

Although these early decisions established the ascendancy of the federal government when a direct conflict arose, the boundary between national and state authority to tax and to regulate commerce remains a no man's land through which the Supreme Court is constantly trying to pick its way. The variety of potential conflicts makes generalizations relatively useless. The court, for example, has long held that a state may not place an 'undue burden' on interstate commerce nor levy a tax on the privilege of engaging in it. Yet as late as 1974 the court could be presented with this modern-dress version of the ancient problem: Is a company which operates an oil pipeline from New York to Texas liable to pay taxes to Louisiana, in which one of the pumping stations is located?

As early as 1851 the court recognized that 'whatever subjects of this [commerce] power are in their nature national, or admit only of one uniform system or plan of regulation, may justly be said to be of such a nature as to require exclusive legislation by Congress.' (*Cooley v. Board of Port Wardens.*) In navigation and aviation, for example, uniform national standards are indispensable. Yet to the states it may not always be clear that they are precluded from exercising any concurrent authority. Even though the national government has adopted comprehensive aviation regulations, some states may presume to ban supersonic planes from their airports by means of anti-noise or anti-pollution laws.

All is not conflict, however. Some concurrent powers are shared quite harmoniously with the national government. In a single elementary school, the textbooks may be bought by state funds and the children's lunch by federal funds. The cost of an interstate telephone call is regulated by federal law, while that of a call between two places in the same state is set by a state commission. If it thus sometimes costs less to phone across the country than within a state, such anomalies are the price of federalism.

Despite national supremacy, the states play a role in the lives of their citizens which is far from inconsequential. Some states are larger in population and size than many European countries. (California has 20 million inhabitants.) Except for foreign relations, each state exercises powers nearly comparable with national governments elsewhere. Each enacts its own criminal and civil laws and enforces them with its own police and judiciary. The vast majority of criminal prosecutions in the United States are undertaken in state courts for the violation of state laws; most prisoners in the U.S. are incarcerated in state institutions. It is the state which solemnizes marriage and sanctions divorces, which charters business corporations, and levies purchase taxes. The states bear primary responsibility for operating and supporting educational systems extending from kindergarten through university graduate schools. The states are the main disbursers of social service benefits and builders of roads, public housing and recreational facilities.

Whatever confusion and inefficiency fifty different legal codes may entail, the diversity of state governments is useful as well as merely traditional. Besides bringing government 'closer to the people', the states serve as isolation laboratories for experiments in public policy. One state may outlaw abortions, another make them freely available. The results of these alternative policies may be judged without having to send the whole country precipitously down one or the other path. Many governmental innovations, such as elections to 'recall' unpopular officials and ombudsmen to oversee administration, began in one state and spread by the force of example. In times of emergency, state initiative can be important: during the Arab oil embargo of 1973–4, one state, Oregon, devised a simple rationing system based on car registration numbers that was widely copied.

Despite their broad discretion and occasional inventiveness, however, the states have undergone a long, steady decline from vigorous independence towards dependence on the national government, whose functions and responsibilities have grown correspondingly. Although the constitution left the states substantial powers, they have not always chosen to use them very creatively or purposefully, and the vacuum caused by the failure of leadership at the state level has invited intervention by Washington. Some problems requiring government solutions, moreover, have grown too large, both physically and financially, for the states individually to cope with them.

A main cause of the states' failure is their political institutions. These differ from one state to another in many details, but all states resemble – indeed, set the model for – the national government in possessing a bicameral (except for Nebraska) legislature, an executive branch headed by a popularly elected governor, and a judicial branch. Unlike the national government, however, most state governments are thoroughly dominated by the legislature, which controls spending and taxation. Governors are relegated to a secondary role, possibly because they have no foreign affairs to conduct and no armed forces (except for a part-time militia) to command. There would be nothing unsound in this arrangement, were it not that the legislatures are often irresponsible, inefficient, corrupt, or all three.

Compared with Congress, the state legislatures attract few able and distinguished persons, their leadership is even less statesmanlike, and because of the relative inattentiveness of the mass media they function without the same glare of publicity. Often the long hegemony of a single party has left the state without an effective opposition. Many state legislators, moreover, conceive of themselves as agents of the localities they represent, rather than as trustees of the state's welfare, and make it their chief duty to exact from the treasury as much as they can for their home towns. Much of the legislative session is taken up by 'logrolling', in which the members support each others' efforts to pass bills bestowing largesse upon their constituencies. Until the reapportionment of the 1960s, moreover, cities were so under-represented in the legislatures that rural and small-town representatives, those most immune to the spread of new ideas, tightly controlled the proceedings.

The venality of state legislatures is legendary. They may have reformed somewhat since the late nineteenth century, when Lord Bryce described proceedings in the New York and Pennsylvania legislatures as 'such a Witches' Sabbath of jobbing, bribing, thieving and prostitution of legislative power to private interest as the world has seldom seen.' But they are still hardly paragons of virtue. The root of the evil is the diffi-

culty of holding any particular member of the legislature
responsible for awarding bonanzas to private interests – a
member may sell his vote without remorse if the rest go along
– combined with the fact that states are often dominated by a
few great corporations that can offer legislators lavish temptations. The munificence of mining corporations may have
something to do with the reluctance of some states to enact
regulations to protect the health of miners and of the environment.

The legislatures are so little trusted that most state constitutions drastically restrict their activities in the apparent
belief that the less done by the lawmakers the better. To tie
their hands, the constitutions often contain hundreds of
thousands of words, prescribing state policies in minute
detail. They may specify the allowable uses for gasoline taxes,
the restrictions on foreclosing mortgages, the formula for allocating school aid and other matters which might have been
left to the legislature. The constitutions, which were pro-
mulgated by conventions (some of them held in the last
century), generally can be amended only by a referendum. In
some states the legislature puts proposed amendments on the
ballot at every election. In recent years, attempts have been
made in most states to draft new constitutions or to substantially revise the old ones in order to give the legislature
more discretion. But a number of new constitutions have been
turned down by the voters, evincing the traditional suspicions.

Some state constitutions hobble the lawmakers by limiting
the time they may spend in session. Although annual meetings
are now usual, until recently many legislatures met only every
other year. Each session may be restricted to a fixed period.
(In Alabama it is merely thirty-six days.) Among the more important powers of the governor is the ability to convene special
sessions, but even these may be constitutionally limited in
duration. Infrequent and short legislative sessions often produce the opposite of the desired result, however. Many laws

manage to get passed, but in the haste to meet the adjournment date few of them get due consideration.

The legislature might be more dynamic and responsive if the executive branch were stronger, but most constitutions have ensured a weak, unco-ordinated executive by providing for the direct election of the principal officers who serve with the governor. The attorney general, the comptroller (treasurer), the secretary of state, and other important figures in the administration are elected independently and may be of different parties. The governor is thus not fully master of his cabinet. Political bickering among members of the executive often makes it ineffective as a counterweight to the legislature.

There are indications that the traditional pattern of legislative ineffectualness and irresponsibility may be changing. The rural–urban imbalance has been righted, and the legislative chambers are increasingly peopled with more energetic young persons, women and blacks. Many states have taken steps to streamline legislative procedures and introduce modern budgetary and fiscal management techniques. State governments have begun to show a greater interest in such pressing problems as conservation, consumer protections and urban redevelopment.

But while new blood and new methods may restore some of the importance of the states, they are unlikely to reverse entirely the trend of 200 years. Many problems are too large in geographical extent to be dealt with by a single state. For any one of them to remedy air pollution, it would be necessary to make the clouds stand still. Crime increasingly requires national solutions. When bank robbers and kidnappers forty years ago acquired cars that could quickly remove them from a state's jurisdiction, a federal law against these malefactors, enforceable by the Federal Bureau of Investigation, became necessary. Today, nationwide organized crime syndicates defy effective state law enforcement, placing the burden on the federal government.

More importantly still, economic life has simply outgrown state boundaries. It would make little sense for each state independently to attempt to deal with monopolistic practices, trade union organization, and fluctuations in the business cycle that are national in extent.

Besides suffering from relatively narrow jurisdictions, the states are hampered by a much more meagre revenue base than the federal government. In 1971, the federal government had revenues of 203 billion dollars, while all the states together had but 140 billion in income, 16 per cent of which came from the federal government in the form of subsidies. The demand for social services, education, housing, roads, and law enforcement have simply overwhelmed the states' financial resources, which depend largely upon relatively static property and purchase taxes. The bulk of federal revenues, in contrast, derives from personal and corporate income taxes, which increase in proportion to economic growth. The discrepancy between the revenue-producing capacities of the two levels of government appears ironical in hindsight, since the constitution originally allowed the national authorities to levy, besides excises and customs, only uniform *per capita* taxes, thus precluding a graduated income tax. Had this provision not been abolished by the Sixteenth Amendment in 1913, because of fears of national insolvency, Washington might have needed subsidies from the states.

The states today naturally turn to the federal government for the solution of any problem that requires a great deal of money. The traditional method of channelling federal resources to the states has been grants-in-aid awarded for purposes specified by Congress. In the nineteenth century, the grants often were in the form of federal lands, which the states might sell for the proceeds. The 'land-grant colleges', forerunners of the state universities, were funded in that way. There are now more than 1000 federal grant programmes for social services, health, education, law enforcement, highways and airports, conservation, and other purposes.

The grant system has spurred state governments into action while allowing them to operate their own programmes. Were the grants not available, it might have fallen to the federal government by default to undertake these programmes directly. In helping those who help themselves, grants also set a minimum national standard for public services, alleviating somewhat the inequalities between richer and poorer states. Mississippi still spends less than half of what New York does for each schoolchild, but the disparity would be even greater without federal education funds.

The grant system can, however, be coercive and foster dependency. Induced by the promise of federal funds to undertake programmes which it does not really want or wants less than others, a state's priorities may be distorted to match those of Congress. Since most grants stringently limit the discretion of the recipients (they are accompanied by thick manuals of regulations), it is difficult not to sympathize with state administrators who complain that bureaucrats in far-off Washington, unfamiliar with local conditions, have denied them necessary flexibility.

To prevent the states from deteriorating into little more than disbursing agents for the national government, some funds have been provided in recent years in the form of 'block grants', which give state authorities more freedom to allocate the money according to their own estimates of local needs. A block grant system was used, for example, in the Omnibus Crime Control Act of 1968 to provide subsidies for state law enforcement.

The most radical approach to ending the client status of the states was embodied in the General Revenue Sharing Act of 1972, which authorized the transfer of $30 billion to state and local governments, during a five year experimental period, with virtually no strings attached. Washington established broad 'priority areas', such as public safety, transportation and environmental protection, but left the actual decisions about spending the money to the recipients. Only about one third of the money goes to state governments; the remainder is allocated to more than 38,000 municipalities, counties, townships and Indian tribes. This 'pass through' system reflected the belief of many in Congress that the states, left to their own devices, would neglect the needs of the cities and the minority groups who live in them.

Congress thus demonstrated a strange ambivalence towards the states. While ostensibly trying to revitalize them, it did not trust them to distribute the money fairly. By transferring the bulk of the funds directly to local governments, in fact, Congress seemed to confirm the irrelevance of the states. Because they are the only sub-national units of government recognized by the constitution, the states have always been regarded as necessary intermediaries between the national and local levels. But since they now seem too small to be efficient and too large to allow much popular participation, their position has been undermined. If revenue sharing, which affords local government a source of sustenance independent of the state legislatures, does achieve its professed goal of creating a 'new federalism', it will most likely be a federalism which displaces the states and brings local government into an immediate relationship with Washington.

This transformation would represent a long overdue recognition of the role of the great conurbations in the life of the nation. Since only 4 per cent of the population was non-rural at the time the constitution was written, it is hardly surprising that cities are not even mentioned in it. But today, when three quarters of all Americans live in cities of more than 50,000 persons, there is hardly any excuse for pretending that the states are the only entities that matter in the federal system and that states adequately represent and protect the interest of the cities within their jurisdictions. Cities have, in fact, suffered consistently from the neglect or outright hostility of state governments.

Continuing inattention to the needs of the cities has allowed their problems to reach crisis proportions. Most of America's larger cities exhibit decaying downtown business centres, inadequate housing, insufficient mass transportation, intense car congestion, and suffocating air pollution. They suffer from increasing rates of crime, violence and drug addiction. Vast tracts have become ghettos inhabited by poor blacks and 'hispanics' (Spanish-speaking Americans). A large proportion of each city's population consists of persons, mainly children, who are more or less permanently dependent upon public welfare funds. (About one million of New York City's eight million inhabitants received welfare benefits in 1975 at a cost of more than $1,360,000,000.) The cities, moreover, have been plagued by racial antipathies which have sometimes turned their schools into battlefields.

At the same time, the tax base on which the city depends has been shrinking as the white middle class and many business enterprises, fleeing the problems of urban life, move to the suburbs. A vicious circle is created: a shortage of revenue leads to poorer services, which drives out more taxpayers and makes revenue even scarcer. Borrowing heavily to meet their expenses, some cities are upon the verge of bankruptcy.

Not only are the financial resources of the city inadequate, but its political institutions are not equal to the responsibilities placed upon them. Legally, a city is a mere creature of the state government, which may amend the charter of incorporation at will. The city has no powers other than what the state legislature chooses to give it. The degree of 'home rule' that the city enjoys, the form of government it has and the types and amounts of taxes that cities may levy are determined by the state. State governments, unfortunately, have been less than generous. When big-city mayors journey, cap in hand, to the state capital (usually located in a small town) in search of appropriations or taxing authority, they often as not meet with indifference.

To rural Republicans, who long dominated and are still powerful in many state legislatures, the city is a hotbed of sin, corruption and Democrats. They care not to pave the devil's streets. Their distaste harks back to the late nineteenth century, when millions of immigrants from southern and eastern Europe arrived there. The earlier, assimilated immigrants from the British Isles and northern, Protestant Europe regarded the urban melting pot as a cauldron of strange tongues, alien religious practices and outlandish customs.

The most repugnant custom of all was the immigrants' tendency to acquire political power by building a 'machine'. The machine was a political organization, ruled by a 'boss', which dispensed patronage – mainly public jobs – in return for the voters' support of designated candidates in city council, mayoral and other elections. The boss and his lieutenants in the various neighbourhoods could also help their clients find their way through the bureaucratic maze of government; if there was trouble with the police, one knew where to turn. For the poor, non-English-speaking immigrant, machine politics was simply a means of survival in a strange land. Looking back from this era of distrusted politicians, it seems almost like a golden age when the political process was immediately relevant to people's lives.

But to the native sons who ran the state legislature, machine politics reeked of corruption. Considering it a manifestation of ignorance and unfamiliarity with American ways, they attempted to reform the cities by educating the new citizens in the elements of 'good government'. In the meantime, however, the legislators thought it prudent to contain the evils of bossism by curtailing the power of city government while it was in the hands of the machine. Thus were produced charters which sharply limited the taxing and spending powers of cities and, typically, divided authority between the mayor and numerous independent boards and commissions.

The circumstances which called forth these niggardly charters no longer exist in most cities. The immigrants have been assimilated, and few of the old-style bosses remain. The descendants of those immigrants, not needing the favours of bosses, have themselves joined in the reform movement in many places. Yet the cities still suffer from the heritage of enfeeblement.

The obvious remedy would have been for the cities to take control of the state legislature through their representatives and enact more favourable terms for urban government. However, rural Republicans often kept control, even though the population balance had shifted to the Democratically controlled cities, because of malapportionment. In a malapportioned legislature, the populous urban parts of the state would have disproportionally fewer seats than would the thinly populated rural areas. The disparities between constituencies could be enormous. In Connecticut, for example, some members of the lower legislative chamber represented 424 times as many constituents as other members; in theory, about 12 per cent of the state's population could elect a majority of the chamber's members. Urban dwellers in Connecticut and elsewhere complained that cows were better represented than people in the legislature.

Malapportionment was a sin of deliberate omission. Electoral district boundaries which, in some cases, dated from the nineteenth century continued to be in use well past the middle of the twentieth. Often the apportionment of seats was mandated by the state's original constitution, assuming thereby an aura of immutability. A Democratic governor of New York in the 1920s remarked ruefully that the state was 'constitutionally Republican'. While the district lines remained frozen in time, enormous population movements from country to city and from overseas into the cities had occurred. But the rural Republicans – and in southern states rural Democrats – paid little heed to census returns whose implication was that power ought to be transferred to urban Democrats. Welded into place by old apportionments, they refused to vote changes in boundaries which could only diminish their numbers and influence.

Their power finally began to crumble in 1964, when urban dwellers successfully invoked the judicial power of the national government to force new apportionments. The Supreme Court held that grossly unequal legislative districts denied inhabitants of the more populous constituencies 'equal protection of the laws' as required by the Fourteenth Amendment. The court proclaimed the doctrine of 'one man, one vote', which necessitated distributing seats in both houses of a legislature in accordance with the principal of population equality. The argument that distinctive geographical and economic interests or traditional political units, like counties, deserved some weight in the formulae of representation was rejected.

During the late 1960s, under actual or threatened federal court orders, all of the state legislatures were reapportioned. But the result was bitterly ironic for the cities. For a good deal of the nominally 'urban' population had moved after the Second World War to the suburban fringes. Most of these displaced urbanites were refugees from city life and, like most refugees, had rather unpleasant memories of their erstwhile place of persecution. The suburban residents also were richer, on the average, than those they left behind and, consequently, tended to convert to Republicanism. Thus, when the legislative districting was reformed, much of the non-rural gain in seats accrued to the suburbs, which were just as Republican and just as anti-urban as the rural areas. Finding common ground in their antipathy to the cities, the rural and suburban legislators coalesced to keep urban interests in subjection.

This is all the more unfortunate in that the suburbs themselves are among the factors contributing to the urban dilemma. For the city and the suburbs together form a great metropolitan organism, an economic and social unit. People may live in one and work in the other; certainly the suburbs would not exist without the commercial heartland of the city to nurture them. Yet the powers of the city government terminate at the city limits. Beyond them, numerous expressions of suburban self-government, such as villages and townships, proliferate. Taken as a whole, the New York City metropolitan area sprawls across three states, twenty-two counties, and about 1400 units of local government. The government of New York City proper is but one of these units.

The obstacles to coherent administration presented by this patchwork quilt must be apparent. The provision of housing, transportation networks, educational facilities or a water supply is complicated by the need to secure agreement among numerous village plenipotentiaries. Even more fatal to rational planning is what Professor Robert Wood has termed the 'segregation of resources and needs'. The cities become increasingly populated by the poor, the suburbs by the rich. Among the suburbs themselves, some are enclaves of the affluent few, others more densely populated but less wealthy. Since the public services of each village and town are supported by what can be raised from local property taxes, the rich communities enjoy such benefits as well-endowed public schools, while the city and the poorer suburbs must make do with more spartan facilities.

Besides segregating resources from needs, the balkanized metropolis segregates whites from blacks. Some cities became predominantly black within the decade of the 1960s because of the white exodus to the suburbs. To help overcome the effects of residential apartheid within the city, federal courts have ordered white pupils bussed to all-black schools and vice versa. But the goal has not been achieved, because most of the white students in many metropolitan areas have taken shelter beyond the city limits. Too few remain to allow anything approaching racial balance in the schools. Hopes of exchanging students between the black city schools and the white suburban schools were dashed by the Supreme Court in 1974, when it ruled that suburban schools in most cases could not be compulsorily included in urban desegregation schemes.

The solution for many of these problems would be a single metropolitan government encompassing both needs and resources. In a few cities, notably Miami and Minneapolis-St Paul, metropolitan governments not unlike the Greater London Council have been established. But elsewhere suburbanites, through their influence in the legislatures, have clung to that rugged independence which, like their lawns and trees, symbolizes the small-town American past that they left the city to recapture.

However, while urban interests are submerged in state politics, they are becoming increasingly salient in the deliberations of Congress. Congressmen from large cities now constitute an important bloc, which has become more conscious of its power and more determined to use it to secure federal remedies for urban ills. One result of this new militancy was the 1974 act that provided capital improvement grants and operating subsidies for mass transit. Previously, national transportation outlays had gone almost exclusively for highways, a policy which benefited rural areas and made possible the very existence of commuter suburbs dependent upon cars. For the city, road building did virtually nothing except gorge its streets with cars and require the demolition of entire neighbourhoods to make high-speed corridors for passing vehicles. But while the mass transit subsidy gave some encouragement to the cities, they are still a long way from persuading the national government to fully shoulder the urban burden which the states have been so unwilling to accept. Until that happens, the cities are likely to remain the stepchildren of the federal system.

4 The Protean Presidency

That the modern Presidency has grown from meagre constitutional beginnings testifies to the energy of the men who held the office and to the severity of the crises during which the country sought salvation in a strong executive. Among the most powerful persons the world has known the President in 1975 presided over 3 million civil servants, disbursed a budget of $350 billion, and commanded an armed force of a million men with an atomic arsenal. Yet he is subject to the rules of office laid down in a document written in the eighteenth century to govern a small, rural nation. The office has acquired power by usage while staying more or less within the spirit of the original document's system of checks and balances. If there is a 'genius of the constitution', the office of President is one of its outstanding products.

The President remains, as Woodrow Wilson observed, 'at liberty both in law and conscience to be as big a man as he can' because the constitution is characteristically laconic about his powers. Before devoting most of its text to stipulating how the President shall be elected, sworn in, paid, and if necessary impeached, Article II does mention that the 'executive power shall be vested in a President'. But what does 'executive power' consist of? Many seemingly executive functions have already been granted to Congress in Article I, including the authority to regulate commerce, declare war, and levy taxes.

The vagueness of the framers has left the Presidency to become whatever circumstances demanded, the merest hints in constitutional wording serving as justification. More details might have denied the flexibility which allowed the President to become today chief executive, legislative leader, head of state, leader of his party, supreme diplomat and chief warrior.

Although the military role has become suspect because of presidential exploits in Southeast Asia, these customary powers have won a grudging acceptance.

Although, according to the organizational chart, the President heads the huge federal bureaucracy, his responsibilities as chief executive exceed his real powers. His supposed subordinates are frequently insubordinate, requiring political rather than managerial skills to keep them in line. This paradox prompted President Harry S. Truman's remark about his future successor, General Eisenhower: 'Poor Ike – it won't be a bit like the Army. He'll find it very frustrating.'

A large part of the bureaucracy, comprising the agencies under an independent commission or board, removes from the President's direct control a vast range of policy matters, including atomic energy (Nuclear Regulatory Commission), civil aviation (Civil Aeronautics Board), telecommunications (Federal Communications Commission), industrial relations (National Labor Relations Board), railroad transport (Interstate Commerce Commission), banking (Federal Reserve Board), securities (Securities and Exchange Commission), scientific research (National Science Foundation), and maritime affairs (Federal Maritime Commission). The President could try to disclaim all responsibility for what happens in those fields, but another Truman epigram, 'The buck stops here', holds true. If the stock exchange were to go bust, the chief executive would have difficulty diverting the public's rancour away from himself and towards the SEC. The difficulty is that the President has some, but not all, of the authority he needs. In dealing with inflation the President can order a wage and price freeze, but the bank interest rate, a crucial economic determinant, is controlled by the Federal Reserve Board, whose members are notoriously autonomous.

The President influences the policy of the independent agencies by nominating the commissioners. But because of their lengthy terms, which exceed the President's, he may be unable to name more than a fraction of any commission. The concurrent power of the Senate to confirm the nominees, moreover, narrows the President's choice to those men who reflect his own views *and* could survive the confirmation hearings. Furthermore, the heady atmosphere of fixed tenure often makes a commissioner change the well-known policy views which led the President to name him. But a President is stuck with his appointees no matter how refractory they become. President Nixon quarrelled over the bank rate with his former trusted economic adviser, Arthur Burns, whom he had appointed chairman of the Federal Reserve Board.

The President is plagued by insubordination not only in the independent agencies, which are after all intended to be insulated from direct political influences, but in his own cabinet as well. Unlike the British cabinet, which is invariably a collection of important party figures, the President's cabinet may be composed of men selected primarily for their help or loyalty to him personally or even for their obscurity (if the post is considered too politically sensitive for any person of known opinions). For reasons of party unity or prestige, the President may include a figure of importance in his own right: perhaps one of the presidential hopefuls who succumbed in the primary elections or the governor of an important state. Should the cabinet member prove uncooperative, the President can, by 'freezing' him out of the inner councils, force him to resign. But resignations in anger carry political costs for the President – no principle of collective responsibility restrains the ousted member – and the chief executive is likely to soldier on with an intransigent running the Department of Agriculture rather than risk an embarrassing departure.

Lacking effective levers for manipulating the bureaucracy he nominally heads, the President relies on persuasion. His persuasiveness does not depend solely on his force of personality. He can trade his support for the pet projects of a cabinet secretary or agency commissioner. He can hold out enticing prospects of appointment to more desirable posts; the under-secretary of the Interior Department might fancy being ambassador to Venezuela. And the President can, for those who have a political following at home, dole out patronage jobs to supporters. On the darker side of persuasion, the President can threaten to cut departmental budgets, kill favourite programmes, and withhold promotions. The way a President 'orders' his bureaucracy into action smacks more of Byzantine court intrigue than the principles taught in colleges of public administration.

The unwieldy bureaucracy stimulated the rapid rise in the last twenty years of the once tiny staff of the Executive Office of the President. In the privacy of the White House basement and the adjacent Executive Office Building, a staff of advisers, speechwriters, lawyers, troubleshooters and liaison men provides the President with an inner council that can rival the cabinet. When he was nominally only a presidential adviser on foreign affairs, Henry Kissinger substituted for the State Department; a domestic affairs adviser may replace the secretaries of a whole group of departments in the President's confidence. Unlike the often unresponsive bureaucracy, the executive staff supplies advice and intelligence the President feels he can trust and carries out his orders unfailingly. No outside loyalties or departmental 'empire-building' intervene.

The increasing importance of the executive staff conjures the spectre of an elite cadre of officials outside the system of checks and balances. Most executive staff members are not subject to confirmation by the Senate, nor can they be required to appear before a congressional investigating committee, as a cabinet secretary can be. Presidents have often claimed that 'executive privilege', a supposed corollary of separation of powers, precludes prying into the workings of the executive office, but the existence of such a privilege has been hotly disputed. Of course, immunity from outside scrutiny is exactly what the President values in his staff.

A more serious objection is that the executive office can become a presidential Disneyland, peopled by devoted henchmen who assure their chief that his every dream is coming true. Such insularity may leave the President ignorant of outside opinion, the problems of the real world and even the activities of his staff. The moral of the Watergate episode surely is that excessive reliance on a 'palace guard' can be a dangerous form of myopia.

Watergate also illustrated the great versatility of a presidential staff, which apparently can include specialists in everything from economic affairs to breaking and entering. The departments headed by cabinet secretaries are created and fixed by statute, but the executive staff can be freely reorganized by the President without authorizing legislation. By quickly establishing White House councils on environmental pollution, consumer protection, cost of living and similar issues of sudden urgency the President seems to be responding to public demands for vigorous action.

The most important of the staff divisions is the Office of Management and Budget, charged with presenting to Congress a single, co-ordinated budget for the entire government. By concentrating the power of allocating funds, the President has enormously increased his control over the departments. A massive, complex document, the budget is so difficult to amend after completion, that a bureaucrat must come hat in hand to the office in advance, pleading his case. In exchange for his allocation the bureaucrat must promise *quid pro quo*. So effective is OMB in augmenting presidential power that Congress in 1975 voted to subject the appointment of the director and assistant-director to senate confirmation.

The politics of the budget reveal how blurred are the lines that theoretically separate the legislative and executive powers. Although Congress, exercising the 'power of the purse', appropriates money, it is up to the chief executive to spend it. The President attempts to force the hand of Congress by preparing a budget request so detailed that even amendments in committee become difficult. Congress nevertheless manages to give the President less money than he asks for in some budget items and more than he asks for in others. (House and Senate committees now co-ordinate budget matters, presenting a united front.)

Cutting the President's funds is generally an effective means of congressional control, except that, as Vietnam proved, the President apparently can run a medium-sized war out of petty cash. Giving the President more than he wants is not a very satisfactory instrument of control. Even if the President were bound to dispose of the entire allocation – which would make the bureaucratic spending mentality compulsory – legislators could not depend on very enthusiastic implementation of the funded programme. The House Armed Services Committee in the 1960s failed to nudge the Defense Department into building an atomic aircraft carrier – the committee chairman's idea of the ultimate weapon – by voting unwanted millions for the project.

President Nixon thwarted congressional munificence by refusing, as an economy measure, to spend billions of the health, education and welfare appropriation. This so-called 'impounding' of money willingly voted makes nonsense of the framers' intention to keep the purse strings tightly in the grip of the legislature. The American forefathers, pre-occupied with the sufferings of Parliament under free-spending monarchs, apparently put the checks in the wrong place. The constitutional validity of presidential impoundment is still uncertain, but Congress in 1974 acted to restrict by law the President's ability to withhold funds.

Although the constitution clearly vests the 'executive power' in the President it was much less specific about his legislative role. Article II stipulates that the President 'shall from time to time give to the Congress information of the state of the union and recommend to their consideration such measures as he shall judge necessary and expedient'. The annual event, more pomp than substance, which the State of the Union Message has become, celebrates the importance of presidential wisdom to Congress. Less well known than this televised ceremonial address to the joint assembly of House and Senate are the special messages on crime, education and foreign aid and the detailed bills which the President may regularly 'recommend to their consideration'. Taken together, the outpouring of suggestions dominates the congressional agenda and makes the President by far the major source of proposed legislation. So addicted are they to presidential stimuli that, when the proposals are delayed, the legislators may complain that they simply cannot get organized.

The proportion of the President's programme enacted is regarded as an indicator of his overall success in office. *Congressional Quarterly*, which keeps score of roll-call votes for Capitol Hill connoisseurs, identifies every aye or no vote as a vote for or against the President. (Rarely does the White House take no position.) By this standard, any sober re-assessment of the Kennedy Administration must conclude that he was not particularly effective; President Johnson, although seemingly less popular, was by comparison a smashing success in gaining congressional approval for his bills.

Although a President may have the initiative in firm grasp, he by no means has a legislative majority under his whip, as a British Prime Minister automatically does, to ensure passage of a bill. A President does not hold office by virtue of being the leader of a dominant parliamentary party. Many Presidents, particularly Republicans in recent decades, have faced a Senate and House solidly controlled by the opposition. It is a handicap, no doubt, but not a crippling infirmity, because neither party in Congress is sufficiently unified to create simple partisan confrontations. Virtually all bills are passed or defeated by a bi-partisan coalition; the President's identification with the minority party thus does not condemn him to perpetual defeat. But it does, obviously, make life harder for him.

On the other hand, if he lacks an assured majority, the President hardly need worry about a unified and well-led opposition. There is no official leader of the opposition, in the British sense, and usually not even a single figure of national prominence approaching the President's. A presidential hopeful may emerge from Congress to claim the right of reply to a televised presidential speech, but often as not the networks are at a loss to know which politician qualifies as an opposition spokesman.

The dominant party in the House and Senate elect majority leaders, but they may have been chosen for their innocuous neutrality among party factions or for their effectiveness in day-to-day legislative routine. Few members of the public could recall the names of the majority leaders if asked. Although the legislative leaders cannot hope to compete with the President in mobilizing public opinion, they have begun to take steps recently to formulate a co-ordinated legislative programme as an alternative to the President's agenda. Lacking the prestige and focus of the Presidency however, it will be difficult to do anything more than react to White House initiatives.

The President's basic resource in promoting his legislative programme is his ability to bargain with some legislators. He may arrange a deal by promising support for their favourite bills and perhaps patronage appointments in return for approving his measures. The President's prestige alone, especially if he has just been elected by a margin sizeable enough to be called a mandate, may convince some legislators to go along. Flattery is also a powerful persuader; the chosen few congressmen relish being photographed on their way to presidential 'briefings' and White House breakfasts, where they are taken into the President's confidence over coffee and eggs. For the obdurate, the President's congressional relations advisers may recommend 'armtwisting', applying pressure by hinting at dire consequences for non-co-operation.

The President's most potent bargaining counter is his constitutional power to veto legislation. A bill becomes law when the President signs it, but, if he disapproves of it, the bill can be returned to Congress with his objections. (If a procrastinating President neither signs it nor returns it within ten days, it becomes law anyway.) The veto may be overcome by passing the bill again, this time by a two thirds vote of both houses instead of a simple majority. Given the difficulty of mustering even simple majorities, the veto is usually fatal. The implicit judgement of the framers that the president's decision ought to prevail over that of 289 representatives and 66 senators – just under two thirds – betrays a certain pessimism about representative democracy. In practice, the veto is exercised sparingly, not because Presidents have no wish to kill numerous bills, but because by doing so they acquire a rather tyrannical image. Occasionally, the President has the opportunity of defeating legislation without a direct rebuff to Congress through the 'pocket veto'. If he refrains from signing a bill, but Congress adjourns before the ten-day time limit has elapsed, the bill becomes defunct.

The veto power would be more effective if it were a scalpel rather than a blunt instrument. Since a bill either must be signed or vetoed in its entirety, the President cannot surgically excise the paragraphs he dislikes, allowing the rest to become law. He must simply take it all or leave it all. Congressmen thus can append 'riders', provisions extraneous to the ostensible purpose of the bill. A President eager to set his seal on important tariff legislation may find himself reluctantly approving construction of a hydro-electric dam in Wyoming as well. Although these package deals hardly contribute to the coherence of legislation, the only alternative is to allow an 'item veto' of individual provisions. That would require a constitutional amendment.

Constitutional amendments are not subject to the veto power; in fact, the President plays no formal part in the amending process at all, a striking omission considering how much importance is attached to his judgement in the framing of legislation.

One source of 'legislative' power that the President has not been able to exploit is his constitutional authority 'on extraordinary occasions' to convene both houses and to adjourn them if they cannot agree on a closing date. Since the authority to convene and adjourn the legislature is one of the bases of executive power in parliamentary systems, it seems strange not to find it in the panoply of presidential powers. The reasons are not hard to discover. Congress meets continuously during about eight months of the year, recessing only for the summer, so there are hardly any 'extraordinary occasions' when the legislators are not already in town. And as the humid Washington heat approaches its August zenith, there is little disagreement about when to adjourn.

The President's authority as commander-in-chief of the armed forces is an explicit constitutional grant amplified by custom. The constitution appoints the President 'commander in chief' of the Army and Navy (the Air Force was understandably overlooked in the eighteenth century) and of the state militias when these reserves, normally commanded by the state governors, are summoned into federal service. A commendable effort to ensure civilian control of the military, this provision has had the paradoxical effect of making generals, from Washington to Eisenhower, seem particularly qualified to be President.

The framers proceeded to muddle the lines of control, however, by granting overlapping military powers to Congress. Only Congress can declare war, authorize military expenditures, conscript soldiers and make rules for regulating the forces. There was an age when a President, learning of an approaching enemy armada, had time to draft a speech asking for a declaration of war. But in the era of hot lines and push-button atomic brinkmanship, the response to military threats must be instantaneous. Consequently, the President has the latitude to deploy forces in such a way that the country is at war *de facto* if not *de jure*. Without a congressional declaration, President Truman sent an army to Korea, President Johnson used the troops to put down a revolution in the Dominican Republic, and both Presidents Johnson and Nixon commanded half a million ground troops and fleets of bombers and ships in Vietnam. Johnson argued that congressional appropriation of military funds for Vietnam was tantamount to a declaration of war, a disingenuous argument at best, since politically it was almost impossible for the legislators, presented with a *fait accompli*, to cut off supplies to 'our boys in the field'. The fact remained that no 'emergency' precluded asking Congress for a declaration at some point in a war which lasted almost a decade. In refusing to seek one, the President simply by-passed the mechanism of checks and balances, raising doubts about the maintenance of constitutional limitations. 'By the early 1970s,' Professor Arthur M. Schlesinger has observed, 'the American President had become on issues of war and peace the most absolute monarch (with the possible exception of Mao Tse-Tung of China) among the great powers of the world.'

'National security' became the universal justification for executive secrecy and the denial of information to Congress, further undermining the legislature's role. Finally, however, Congress roused itself to reassert its authority. It voted in 1973 to deny funds for the extension of military operations into Cambodia and Laos and passed a War Powers Resolution, which explicitly limits the time during which the President can deploy forces in combat without a declaration of war. The resolution also required the President to 'consult' Congress whenever possible before sending troops into combat. Whether Congress, by this assertion, has successfully reclaimed its war powers remains to be seen. In the first significant test of the resolution, the *Mayaguez* incident in 1975, President Ford merely informed congressional leaders, after the fact, that he had ordered an attack on Cambodia to retake the captured vessel. If Presidents can meet their obligation to consult so cheaply, Congress can hardly be said to possess even the power to advise and consent in matters of war and peace.

On rare but significant occasions, the President deploys the forces domestically as well as internationally. The lavishly armed state and city police forces can handle most situations, but Presidents have ordered in troops to put down urban rioting, escort black children to newly desegregated schools, and to sort the mails when the postal workers went on strike. Presidents are loathe to use the army inside the country lest they resemble a banana republic generalissimo and raise questions about the scope of their lawful powers. During the Second World War President Roosevelt, exercising what he assumed to be his domestic military powers, had all Japanese-Americans 'evacuated' from the West Coast to detention camps. The affair is remembered today as a grievous infringement of civil liberties.

The American Presidency unites two roles that parliamentary systems keep separate; head of government and head of state. In British terms, the President is the Prime Minister and the sovereign. The chief of state function is not explicit in the constitution but has been inferred from the President's duty to receive ambassadors. Whatever its origin, the dual role creates precisely the kind of confusion other systems sought to avoid. Watching the President speak on television, the citizen cannot easily distinguish at the moment whether he is seeing the Olympian symbol of his nation or the leader of a partisan administration. That makes it difficult to evaluate the President's words.

The confusion tends to be exploited by a President in order to make support for his policies seem to be the patriotic thing to do. When confronted by strident opposition to his Vietnam policy, President Johnson once reminded his critics: 'I'm the only President you've got.' Converting loyalty to the nation into loyalty for administration policy, known as wrapping oneself in the flag, is much easier in the realm of international relations. Americans feel guilty about carping behind the President's back while he is away representing the majesty of America at the Great Wall of China or the Kremlin. President Nixon was notably more successful when he asked Americans to support him as he negotiated with the Communist powers than when he invoked 'national security' to thwart the investigation of his re-election campaign activities.

Various proposals have been advanced to remove from the President's calendar the trivial duties of the chief of state, among them lighting the national Christmas tree, posing with the Handicapped Child of the Year, and throwing out the first ball at the opening of the baseball season. But obviously a President needs to cultivate his ceremonial image as chief of state, so that he may be higher and mightier in the thick of partisan battle. For every President is mindful that he represents all the power of the United States government but cannot exercise it fully.

The nation needs to speak with a single voice in international affairs, so a President who is chief of state and military commander seems eminently suited to be chief diplomat. The framers gave the President authority to conclude treaties, but added the qualifying phrase 'by and with the advice and consent of the Senate'. Two thirds of the senators must vote to approve any pact which the President negotiates. This incarnation of the checks and balances principle reflects the isolationism of the infant republic, epitomized by George Washington's Farewell Address warning against foreign alliances. Typically it has been the Senate which has registered periodic bursts of isolationist sentiment in America by rejecting treaties. Expressing the post-First World War disillusionment with European rivalries, the Senate refused to approve Woodrow Wilson's Versailles Treaty.

Even when there was no specific treaty to ratify, the Senate has, by extension, kept a watching brief over the President's diplomacy. The Senate Foreign Relations Committee, under Chairman J. William Fulbright, was an early opponent of the war in Vietnam and indeed all foreign commitments surreptitiously given by the President.

Because the Senate can veto them, a President may avoid formal treaties, preferring instead to arrive at an 'executive agreement'. The exchange of destroyers for bases with Britain in 1940 and the provision of military assistance to Vietnam and Thailand in the 1960s were accomplished by an executive agreement. Although it seems a case of treaty-by-another-name, Presidents have succeeded so far in keeping these agreements outside the Senate's jurisdiction. However, most require funding, which affords both the House and Senate some control. Funding the foreign aid programme every two years allows the legislators to express their opinion of particular aspects of presidential policy by well-aimed budget cuts.

Overall, there can be little doubt that the President determines the nation's behaviour in international politics. The names of Presidents Monroe, Truman, Eisenhower and Nixon are linked to 'doctrines' that proclaimed significant policy decisions without the consultation or approval of any other branch of government. The power of war or peace rests in the President's unfettered hands, as anyone who lived through the tense days of the Kennedy–Khrushchev encounter over Cuba in 1962 can attest; the man who holds the trigger inevitably gives the orders. When threatened with external dangers, the complex system of checks and balances reverts to a tribal dependence on the warrior chief.

Besides his duties as chief executive, chief of state, chief diplomat, chief warrior and chief legislator, the President must be chief of his party as well. In parliamentary systems, a politician becomes Prime Minister by being leader of a party. In America, the reverse occurs. By virtue of being elected, the President is thrust into the unofficial position of 'standard bearer' of the party which nominated him. As the most prominent party member, the President must keep his Gallup Poll popularity index high in order that candidates for lesser offices may bask in his reflected glory, and a disastrous party showing in the congressional elections or elections for state governorships may be construed as a symptom of public hostility to the President.

Although both the Republican and Democratic parties are merely loose confederations of state organizations, the President bears ultimate responsibility for maintaining his party's cohesion. He endorses candidates for mayor, Congress and governor, posing with his arm around the contender. Or he may be required to intervene in a dispute splitting a local party. President Kennedy helped the Reform Democrats prevail over their intra-party opponents in New York State by dispensing federal patronage jobs through the leaders of the favoured faction.

Despite his responsibility for keeping the fifty state organizations in fighting trim, the President exerts little influence over the nominations which mean most to him: representatives and senators. Were he able to prevent renomination of legislators, he would command a disciplined block of votes in Congress. But party organizations at the state and congressional district level are so jealous of their independence and so immune from presidential sanctions that he cannot control their choice of candidate. Consequently, the President cannot rely on his own party alone for legislative support. That complicates his task enormously, since he must be both leader of his party *and* a statesman capable of organizing bi-partisan legislative coalitions.

With these several roles to be juggled, the effectiveness of the Presidency may seem to depend upon the personality of the man who fills the office. Certainly his skills, his strengths and weaknesses, his conception of the proper scope of the office are important determinants, but the office responds more to the pull of circumstances than to the force of personality. The office, and the demands put upon it, make the man. Franklin D. Roosevelt was an 'activist' President, but he served during depression and world war; Eisenhower was less energetic but his was an era of relative peace and domestic harmony. The steady expansion of presidential power under all encumbents has reflected the increasing world importance of the United States and the growing number of economic, social and technical problems from inflation to air pollution, that demand national leadership. As the only official elected by the nation as a whole and the country's spokesman to the world, the President is looked to for leadership.

The Presidency has not usurped power; it has been offered up on a silver platter by Congress, which in parlous times is prone to delegate its responsibility to the executive. The reasoning is basically sound. Better able to respond to rapidly changing situations, the President can 'legislate' on behalf of Congress, which has laid down general guidelines. Given the vicissitudes of international economics, it makes sense to allow the President discretionary powers to raise and lower import duties on a range of items from teapots to transistors rather than to pass a new law for each fluctuation in the market. Moreover, even the most detailed regulatory acts require enforcement, and enforcement requires the exercise of executive discretion: Which firms are violating the anti-trust laws? When is it time to increase farm acreage allotments? The mere fact that Congress passes so much regulatory legislation must mean that executive authority is extended as well.

There are limits, however, to the amount of discretion Congress can delegate. Certainly, it could not, in a moment of generosity, grant *all* its powers to the President, thereby instituting a dictatorship. The Supreme Court has traditionally kept vigilant; in the 1930s excessive delegation of power was the ground upon which several New Deal regulatory laws – most notably the National Industrial Recovery Act – were held unconstitutional. The standards for economic regulation were relaxed in later years, but executive actions may still be challenged in court on the ground that too much authority was ceded by Congress or that the President exceeded the authority granted. The suit would be especially pertinent if the executive action impinged upon provisions of the Bill of Rights or the Fourteenth Amendment.

The general, almost imperceptible, slippage of power from legislative into executive hands is a feature of most twentieth-century democracies. In America the slide has not been as sharp as in other countries because the separation of powers has allowed the congressional committees and their staffs to become alternative centres of power. But in a way the potential for executive usurpation is much greater because the President, serving a fixed term, is not vulnerable even theoretically to a vote of no confidence.

The ultimate congressional check upon presidential power is to impeach the President. A bill of impeachment must be voted by a simple majority of the House of Representatives, acting as prosecutor. The Senate then sits as a jury to hear the case. A vote of two thirds of the members present is required for conviction, which removes the President from office. The former President is liable to be tried in the ordinary courts for any crimes he may be accused of committing.

What a President must do to warrant impeachment is a matter of dispute. One school argues that the 'high crimes and misdemeanours' spoken of in the constitution must be actual violations of law. Another school, patronized by many congressmen, contends that whatever misdeeds the House and Senate think sufficiently serious are grounds for impeachment. The danger in the latter theory is the natural tendency of Congress to interpret disagreement with the President as a sign of moral turpitude in the White House. In the only impeachment ever brought to trial, President Andrew Johnson was accused in 1867 of dismissing certain cabinet members against the wishes of Congress. He was acquitted by one vote, a narrow escape that left a strong distaste for the procedure and a presumption that it would never again be invoked.

The initial reluctance of Congress to take up impeachment during the Watergate scandal indicates how painful is the prospect of bringing proceedings against an official of such awesome responsibilities. While the President is in the dock of the Senate, the disruption of government business would be complete (even the international currency markets became fidgety when the prospect of Nixon's impeachment was raised). Moreover, acquittal might not totally vindicate the President, whose capacity to govern for the remainder of his term would be impaired.

Despite these objections, however, Congress did begin the task of impeaching President Nixon when the available evidence left no doubt that he had committed criminal acts. Although the process was aborted by the President's resignation, the decision of the House Judiciary Committee to bring formal charges served notice that the impeachment provision is still a live section of the constitution.

The resignation itself set a political precedent of some significance. Although parliamentary premiers resign as a matter of course when they lose the confidence of the legislature, fixed tenure of office has been a hallmark of the American Presidency. No President had ever resigned the office before, no matter how far his relations with Congress had deteriorated or how besmirched by scandal his name had become. The belief in a President's right to serve out his term is so strong that the main argument offered in support of the pardoning of Nixon was that by having to resign he had already suffered condign punishment.

The irony of impeachment is that the President's hand-picked Vice President succeeds to the office, leaving essentially the same administration in power. But this is only one of several odd features of the Vice Presidency, an institution which can be called the missing link in the constitutional system. A shadowy figure, the Vice President is part of both the executive and legislative branches, although he has no real duties in either. His only responsibility under the constitution is to preside over the Senate, a purely formal task, and to cast the deciding vote when ties occur, which is infrequently. Otherwise he merely waits in the wings in case the President dies, resigns or is removed from office.

Unlike the stand-in actor, however, the Vice President never has a chance to learn the part. Most Presidents have studiously avoided delegating any important administrative or policy making duties to their Vice Presidents. Often the vice presidential candidate is personally picked by the President at the nominating convention because he is thought able to deliver the votes of a section of the country, not because his service is valued. President Kennedy chose Lyndon Johnson as his running mate to attract the 'Southern vote'. After the election, Johnson, once the powerful majority leader of the Senate, went into eclipse until Kennedy was assassinated.

A consequence of vice presidential obscurity is that when a President dies, precisely the moment when the country needs to be reassured about the succession, a virtually unknown and inexperienced figure takes over the reins of government. One proposal for reform would have the President delegate some of his duties to the Vice President as an apprenticeship and take care to keep him well informed about the business of the executive branch. Another suggestion is that the choice of a vice presidential candidate be thrown open to the nominating convention, rather than left to the presidential candidate alone, thereby democratizing the selection process and ensuring that a person of independent stature in the party is chosen.

Some would go further and simply abolish the office of Vice President by constitutional amendment, substituting a special election whenever the Presidency becomes vacant. At the moment, no election follows the death, resignation or removal of a President, no matter how many years remain in his term. It is almost as if the Presidency were a popularly constituted monarchy whose succession crises had been institutionalized in a quadrennial election. When the 'monarch' departs unseasonably, the state is left without a satisfactory method of filling the void.

Even a satisfactory method of replacing Vice Presidents has been difficult to devise, as illustrated by the history of the Twenty-fifth Amendment. Adopted in 1967, it provides that when the Vice Presidency becomes vacant, the President may nominate someone to fill the office with the approval of both houses of Congress. Normally, this would occur when a Vice President succeeds to the Presidency. Few believed that the amendment would be invoked very often, but within the space of fifteen months in 1973–4 two Vice Presidents were chosen. One of these, Gerald R. Ford, eventually succeeded to the Presidency, becoming the first person ever to hold that office without running in a national election.

This series of events brought forth objections that the Twenty-fifth Amendment is fundamentally undemocratic, allowing a President – even one threatened with impeachment for misdeeds – to name his own successor. Since the House and Senate may spend months scrutinizing the credentials of persons nominated for the Vice Presidency, an election for the post could just as well be held, but it might result in a Vice President of a different party than the President's. That was a possible electoral outcome under the constitution as originally drafted. However, the arrangement was soon pronounced unworkable and abolished by the Twelfth Amendment in 1804.

Succession to the Presidency is such a sensitive issue, that even the question of how often a President may succeed himself was finally resolved by amendment. A fear of the autocratic potentiality of the Presidency prompted passage in 1951 of the Twenty-second Amendment, limiting any President to two full terms. But because the President is still in the undignified position of having to run for re-election, both Lyndon Johnson and Richard Nixon suggested a single six-year term, long enough to achieve something yet avoiding the mixing of base electoral politics with high statesmanship. Of course, forbidding re-election also eliminates fear of the electorate, probably the most effective restraint on presidential power. Even the present limitation brands the second-term President as a 'lame duck', the opprobrious epithet of any officeholder whose lack of political prospects renders him dangerously unaccountable.

Is the President, in fact, too powerful? An American's opinion of the proper scope of presidential authority depends on his political bias and his times. In the grip of the Great Depression, liberals hoping to find the Presidency an agency for social reform were frustrated by the limitations of Roosevelt's office. In the early 1970s, faced with a President bent upon curbing the reforming zeal of the executive, they have decried the lack of constitutional restraints and urged Congress to reassert its authority. Conservatives have experienced a similar, though opposite, transformation in their attitude to the Presidency. These alterations have occurred cyclically throughout the history of the republic, and they are likely to continue. The various forms that the controversy takes only demonstrates how readily constitutional philosophy subserves political expediency.

5 Congress: The Legislative Labyrinth

Looking back upon his twenty years in the House of Representatives, Nicholas Longworth, the speaker from 1925 to 1931 remarked ruefully that 'During the whole of that time we have been attacked, denounced. despised. hunted, harried, blamed, looked down upon, excoriated and flayed. I refuse to take it personally.' In the ensuing half century not much has changed; Congress continues to be held in chronically low esteem by its constituents. A poll taken in 1974 reported that only 21 per cent of the public believed that their legislators were performing even adequately. Yet most congressmen, following Longworth's example, are still not taking it personally, at least not enough to make them change fundamentally the behaviour which has made the name of Congress synonymous with ineffectuality.

One reason for its ill repute is that Congress does not seem to get very much accomplished of a positive nature. In an average session, lasting about a year, Congress may pass about fifteen major acts. but scores of other bills become mired at various stages of the legislative process for reasons unrelated to their inherent merit. Some proposals. such as national health insurance, languish for decades. unable to overcome the prodigious obstacles to enactment. Congress. in short, looms as a bastion of negation. Reinforcing that impression, Presidents have often chastised Congress for failing to deal with the agenda which they have set before it while neglecting to produce alternative measures. Congressional inertia is particularly noticeable in times of crisis. Despite energy shortages, economic slumps and environmental menaces, the sleeping giant slumbers on. When Congress does act in an emergency, frequently the only solution it can devise is to give the President virtual blanket authority to deal with the problem as he sees fit – a response which does nothing to evoke admiration for the legislators' creativity.

Collectively, congressmen seem to have a short attention span for important issues. As David S. Broder, a Washington political analyst, has remarked, 'The natural tendency of Congress is to fly off in dozens of directions at once. Every member – and particularly every Senator – wants to do his own thing, a tendency which would be funny were the consequences for the country not so great.' The distractions come with the office. Although Congress has two formal functions, legislating and monitoring the operations of government, congressmen individually have an informal duty, enforced by the desire for re-election, to serve their constituents. The great issues may have to wait while the legislators concentrate on securing a federal grant for improving a highway at home or having a local beauty spot declared a national monument.

Unfortunately, there is no one to check these centrifugal tendencies, because Congress lacks firm, centralized leadership. The President does not hold office by virtue of leading a legislative majority. Quite the contrary, the constitutional separation of executive and legislative powers ensures that the President and members of Congress will spring from different electoral bases, suffer different political risks and generally look at the world from different viewpoints. Very often the President is of the minority party in Congress. From 1945 to 1975, the Democrats controlled Congress in all but two years, but the White House was occupied by a Republican for fifteen years.

If a President is not the natural leader of Congress, the leadership function might be expected to devolve upon the elected heads of the majority party: the speaker of the House and the Senate majority leader. But there can be no effective leadership without some means of coercion, which the party chiefs lack. Their whips have no sting. A member of the British parliament can be coerced, ultimately, by the threat of losing the party designation at election time for having rebelled against the party whip; the national party leadership can affect his chances of being selected by his local party organization. But nomination of candidates for the Senate and House of Representatives is in the hands of state and local party leaders. Even without their support, one can acquire the party label for a congressional campaign merely by running successfully in a primary election.

The party leadership in Congress, moreover, can hardly hope to commit its members to a common legislative programme when each party is a catch-all for a broad spectrum of political leanings. The system prevailing in Congress, in reality, is not two-party politics, but four-party politics among conservative Democrats, liberal Democrats, conservative Republicans, and liberal Republicans. On most issues, *ad hoc* coalitions are formed among these four groupings.

In the absence of centralized leadership, the houses of Congress are controlled by an infra-structure of autonomous standing committees, centres of decision-making which are often referred to as 'little legislatures'. Although not envisioned by the constitution, the committee system is by now a traditional institution, whose existence is usually rationalized by pointing to the need for legislative expertise. After long service in the House Committee on Agriculture, a representative learns enough about crops to scrutinize Agriculture Department officials and farm bills with a knowledgeable eye. The expertise of congressmen on specialized committees and their formidable array of staff resources has helped somewhat to balance the growth of executive power.

Deference to specialists is the strict rule by which committees support each other, and a committee's expert judgement is only rarely, and usually unsuccessfully, challenged from outside. When the Committee on Armed Services kills a defence bill, it is difficult for the other representatives to breathe life into it again. Moreover, since debate in the House is usually quite limited, the version of a bill which is reported to the floor by the committee tends to pass without much amendment. The committees are thus gatekeepers in the legislative process.

While every committee is lord of its domain, three committees of the House are pre-eminent. The Appropriations Committee is powerful for the simple reason that most bills call for expenditures, which it alone can authorize. If revenue is to be raised to meet those expenditures, taxes must be approved by the Ways and Means Committee, another crucial panel. But most powerful is the Rules Committee. Initially intended to serve merely as a legislative traffic director, the committee usually allows its political preferences to colour its scheduling decision. It has been compared, by Professor William H. Riker, to a 'toll bridge attendant who argues and bargains with each prospective customer; who lets his friends go free, who will not let his enemies pass at any price . . .'

Some bills, the committee decides, are of such perfection that they can be sent to the floor under a 'closed rule', a severe limitation on debate which makes it impossible for opponents to offer amendments. A bill that the committee does not favour is scheduled under an 'open rule', permitting opponents to amend it to death, or never scheduled at all. Sponsors of legislation often must make substantive concessions to the Rules Committee in order to have it released. Under a bylaw, a majority of the House can force the committee to schedule a bill by signing a 'discharge petition', but securing 218 signatures – each of them risking retaliation by the committee – is not an easy task. During the 1940s and 1950s, the Democratic majority of the committee was a pillar of southern conservative obstructionism, but in the 1960s, the committee was infiltrated by more liberal members, allies of the speaker. The committee, however, remains alertly posted at the toll bridge.

Although it may contribute to the expertise of the Congress, the committee system allows the majority will to be thwarted by a committee of thirty to forty members – or more precisely the committee's chairman. The chairman schedules meetings, controls the agenda, appoints subcommittees and their chairmen, hires the staff, and spends committee funds running into millions of dollars. Until recently some chairmen ran their committees like feudal baronies. The chairman is powerful because he owes his position not to the support of his committee members nor to the party leadership in the House, but to the automatic operation of the rule of seniority. The majority-party member with the longest tenure on the committee has always been acclaimed chairman by divine right. He has thus been, in the strictest sense of the word, irresponsible.

The seniority system has some virtues. In a legislature which values specialist experience, it elevates the member with the most time on the job. Moreover, it solves the problem of choosing a chairman without inciting bloody political struggles. Since the House must reorganize itself biennially, it could conceivably spend the entire two years in battle over the chairmanships if seniority were not the guiding principle.

However, although it does reduce conflict, the seniority system settles for 'peace at any price'. No effort can be made to choose the most worthy member, for the seniority rule precludes any sort of 'merit' selection. It is not the most dedicated or able member who is chosen, but simply the oldest in service and often in years. Age may confer wisdom, but it generally also breeds conservatism. The gerontocracy which presides over the committee structure is thus more conservative than the Congress as a whole.

The committee chairmen in recent decades have also tended to be more conservative because the seniority system ensured that they came from conservative districts. A congressman acquires seniority by being returned election after election, a consistency which is more probable in the districts where one party is dominant – the 'safe seats'. A large number of such districts are in conservative, rural areas, and many are in the south.

The influence of southern seniority is mathematically self-evident: more than half the chairmen in the House and Senate in the 1973–4 Congress were from the south, although only about a quarter of the population lives there. Arkansas alone, a thinly populated, rustic state, contributed to that Congress the chairmen of the Senate Foreign Relations Committee, the Senate Appropriations Committee and the House Ways and

Means Committee. It is true, of course, that many urban House districts in the north are Democratic safe seats, but the cities have not capitalized on their advantage. Because of the relative poverty of the south and the insignificance of its local politics, talented southern politicians are more likely than their northern brethren to be attracted to Congress as a career. Occupants of northern safe seats abandon them readily to become mayors and state judges. Those urban representatives who do remain in Congress for long periods often treat their positions as sinecures, devoting their real energies to managing political affairs at home and allowing the diligent southerners to become masters of the parliamentary process in Washington.

The seniority system and the committee satrapies trace their roots to a backbench revolt in 1910 against the auto-cratic rule of the House speaker, 'Czar' Joe Cannon. His powers were parcelled out among the committee chairmen, and he was stripped of his right to appoint them, the rule of seniority being substituted. In effect, a tyranny was replaced by an oligarchy. Efforts to reform the House since then have concentrated upon restoring the powers of the speaker, while making him formally responsible to the rank-and-file members of the majority party. Gathering strength during the 1960s, the reform movement effected a series of startling changes at the opening of the ninety-fourth Congress in 1975. Normally, only a small percentage of the representatives fail to return after an election, but the election of November 1974, the first after the Watergate scandal, registered a popular backlash against in-cumbent politicians. It brought to the House seventy-five new Democrats. Committed to institutional reform, this younger and more liberal generation of representatives was unwilling to accept the freshman's maxim that 'to get along, you've got to go along'. The newcomers immediately made their presence felt in the House Democratic Caucus, the party's plenary policy-making body. Three doyens of the southern old boy network, the chairmen of the Committees on Armed Services, Agriculture and Banking – two septuagenarians and an octogenarian – were deposed by a vote of the caucus and replaced by more liberal northerners. The success of the putsch may mean that, although still an important criterion for chairmanships, seniority has lost its status as the exclusive consideration.

The caucus also reformed the method of assigning Democrats to committees. Until 1975, that prerogative had been enjoyed by the Democratic members of the Ways and Means Committee, sitting as a committee on committees, who used it for their own political purposes: building support for their favourite tax bills. The caucus transferred the assignment function to the Democratic Steering and Policy Committee, composed of the House speaker, the Democratic majority leader and a cross-section of the party membership in the House. In the first demonstration of its new power, the Steering and Policy Committee appointed several liberals, some of them freshmen, to the Appropriations and Ways and Means Committees, hitherto strongholds of trustworthy conservatives with at least a decade of seniority. The Democrats thus seemed to be moving towards firmer leadership, under a policy committee responsive to the rank-and-file members, and away from the fragmentation of power among feudal chieftains. That, in turn, has opened up possibilities for a basic legislative programme to which all party members are committed.

Despite the problems inherent in allocating the chairmanships and seats, few doubt that the system of standing committees is necessary. In the House, especially, the size of the membership is too unwieldy to permit extensive deliberation as a whole upon every proposal. It is the committee's task to organize research, hold hearings, and thrash out compromises before a bill comes to the floor. Standing committees are also better able to maintain constant 'legislative oversight' of the executive departments in their special fields of policy. The House Committee on the Interior, for example, keeps watch on the Department of the Interior, examining its budget requests, criticizing administrative decisions and exposing mismanagement. Some bureaucrats spend most of their time preparing answers to congressional inquiries, and cabinet secretaries do not look forward to testifying at hearings, knowing that they may be in for a televised browbeating by a panel of legislators in a vengeful mood. The longevity of a committee chairman ensures that he will know the workings of 'his' agency the way he knows the politics of his home district. Many chairmen have far greater experience in their fields than the cabinet secretaries. Between 1947 and 1975 there were only three chairmen of the House Armed Services Committee while about a dozen Secretaries of Defense came and went.

It would be inaccurate, however, to describe the nexus between the committee and the departments as a wholly adversary relationship. Under normal circumstances, most business between congressional committees and executive offices is transacted in an atmosphere of cosy reciprocity. The committee approves the budgets and policies, making changes here and there, and the bureaucrats are properly deferential to each congressman's dignity and political interests.

Many executive decisions, in fact, are explicable only in terms of what they do for an important congressman's district. Military strategy and the constituency interests of Armed Services Committee chairmen, for example, show a remarkable coincidence. The model of the enterprising congressman was Mendel Rivers, who chaired the committee from 1965 to 1970. By the end of his tenure, his home district in South Carolina boasted eleven major naval installations, including shipyards, missile bases, hospitals and training camps. The Defense Department was spending almost $1000 there annually for every single inhabitant. His successor as chairman managed to have the Bureau of Naval Personnel and the Naval Reserve Headquarters transferred from the capital to his district and installed in a complex of buildings named after himself.

In essence, a three-way relationship exists among department, committee and lobby groups. Although not formally a part of the policy-making process, the lobby groups, representing economic or political interests, play a substantial role. Oil producers, soya bean growers, power-generating companies, car manufacturers, retired persons, veterans and racial minorities are among the groups which maintain lobbies in Washington. Trade unions make their influence felt through lobbying efforts. Even foreign nations, not content to rely on ambassadorial contacts, attempt to sway Congress directly, especially on foreign trade bills, by retaining lobbyists to stalk the halls of the Capitol.

Exactly how much effect lobbying has is not clear, and it probably varies from one group to another. Lobbyists – or at least their clients – apparently believe they are effective for, in 1973, they officially reported spending $10 million on their attempts to influence legislation. That figure, however, is but a fraction of what is really spent. Because of gaping loopholes in the Federal Regulation of Lobbying Act of 1946, many lobbyists avoid filing the required spending reports or, if they do file, carefully understate their outlays. Many of the larger lobbying organizations keep plush offices in the capital and employ large staffs, including former legislators and government officials with contacts in strategic places. Cultivated by lavish wining and dining on tax deductible expense accounts, these contacts are more important than such visible lobby activities as testifying at committee hearings. A friendly congressman can keep a lobbyist informed about the progress of pending bills, and the lobbyist, in turn, can keep him supplied with data, such as industry statistics, to help the legislator champion the lobbyist's cause.

Most lobbyists probably spend their time working with legislators who are already sympathetic, but there is good reason to suspect they are not above making converts where necessary by offering tangible inducements. Lobbies representing large economic interests can afford to 'invest' some of the profits they expect to gain through legislation by contributing to the re-election campaign funds of congressmen. The dairy industry, for example, whose earnings depend on federal pricing policies, has funnelled money from its 'war chest' to the campaigns of more than eighty senators and representatives. While technically legal, such well-distributed baksheesh obviously buys support for the dairymen. Drinkers of milk, meanwhile, are hardly in a position to raise a counter-offer in order to avoid paying a few pennies more for each bottle.

The undue influence of big money confutes the argument that lobbying is nothing more than a healthy manifestation of interest group competition. a part of America's pluralist democracy. Even without the influence of money, though, it is doubtful whether all are equal in the clash of interests. Some lobbies have been lucky or crafty enough to become recognized as the mouthpieces through which *vox populi* speaks. The forestry subcommittee of the House Interior Committee for many years was wont to consult only the envoys of the lumber companies whenever it needed to discover what 'the public' thought about proposed dispositions for the national forests. By the 1970s, however, many of the unorganized and voiceless interests began to recognize the benefits of concerted lobbying. Today the forestry subcommittee's consciousness of the relevant public has been expanded to include the Sierra Club and other environmental conservation groups. A partial solution has also been found for the funding problem that had always hampered non-business lobbies. The example was set by Common Cause, a 'public interest lobby' supported by thousands of small individual subscriptions.

For the lobbyists, blocking a bill is easier than getting one passed, because many bills die of sheer exhaustion along the tortuous route to enactment. A bill may begin life in either house, heralded by some public agitation and supported by a galaxy of lobbies and executive agencies. It may be introduced with the President's blessing or against his will. The bill is first referred to the appropriate committee. Since the jurisdictional boundaries of the committees tend to overlap, a dispute may erupt among several committees claiming the same bill. Some-times these disputes are resolved by simply ignoring the bill. Several thousand bills go to committee each session of

Congress, but only a fraction of them ever return. Most are consigned to limbo, a procedure known as 'pigeon-holing'. The committee will select a few bills that it wishes to consider and hold public hearings. More often than not, the informative value of these hearings is slight: they are stage-managed to mould public support for the views already held by the committee.

The committee then meets in a 'mark-up' session to put the bill into final form. Here, in an atmosphere of intense trading, the members try to reach a compromise among themselves. If the bill can be reported out unanimously, its chances of passage are greatly improved. The version finally reported by the committee may bear little or no resemblance to the bill originally introduced.

The next hurdle is to move the bill on to the floor. Since the calendar is crowded, time for debate is at a premium. A bill which is 'called up' early stands a better chance than one scheduled later, because the chamber may fail to complete its agenda before the Congress expires. (The life span of a Congress is two years.) All unconsidered bills remaining must retrace their steps in the next Congress. Control of the House calendar is in the hands of the Rules Committee and, to some extent, the speaker. In the Senate, the majority leader determines the order of debate.

The floor debate is rarely a model of parliamentary give-and-take. The members make speeches at each other, and few minds are ever changed by the outpouring of rhetoric. Most of the words printed in each day's *Congressional Record* were never even uttered on the floor. Since congressmen speak primarily 'for the folks back home', they considerately place their orations into the record without forcing their colleagues to listen to them. Probably the chief purpose served by the debate is to provide an indication of legislative intent to guide the courts in interpreting the act. However, significant amendments, either strengthening or weakening a bill, sometimes may be voted during the debate, and the bill's sponsors may engage in 'horse-trading' to win enough votes for passage.

The first question a congressman must ask himself about any bill is whether to vote at all. Absenteeism may be the better part of valour if the legislator is caught between his personal opinions and his constituents' demands. He can also escape the dilemma by means of a voice vote, in which ayes and no's are shouted in unison. But any member may demand a roll-call, in which everyone's vote is recorded.

Since a bill moves through the Senate and the House independently, it can fail in either place. If it is passed by both chambers, the two versions may be quite divergent. Although the constitution neglected to provide for such discrepancies, an institution known as the 'conference committee' has evolved for the purpose of reconciling bills. The speaker of the House and the Senate majority leader each appoint a team of 'managers' to the conference committee, which may meet in closed session. Often the only way for the committee to resolve the differences is to draft an entirely new bill. The bill reported back to both houses by the committee is normally accepted in a floor vote without further ado because of the pressure to get some kind of bill passed. The final version, approved by the House and Senate, is sent to the President, who has three options open to him. He can sign it into law, he can veto it, or he can allow it to go into law unsigned by merely leaving it on his desk for ten days. A veto may be overridden by a two thirds vote of each house, but that much support is not easily obtained.

Given this complicated process, it may be hard to imagine how any laws are ever enacted. A bill may succumb at the committee stage, on the floor, in conference committee, or in the White House. Those that succeed are significantly altered by compromises – so much so that their original sponsors may oppose the final version. Compromise is the *modus operandi* of the Congress; most congressmen believe that some kind of bill, however deficient, is better than no bill at all. This half-a-loaf philosophy does not always produce legislation which is effective or coherent or even self-consistent. It sacrifices principle on the altar of consensus. But at least the framers of the constitution must be congratulated on having fashioned a system which avoided their chief bugaboo, the spectre of one faction taking control and running amok.

Although much elaborated by their heirs, the built-in negative bias of the legislative press was part of the framers' scheme for inhibiting legislative activism. The simple fact that Congress was divided into two chambers and given differing bases of representation laid the groundwork for stalemate. The House was to be the popularly elected chamber and presumably the most radical and headstrong. The Senate was to be almost an international council, each state's two ambassadors sitting on terms of sovereign equality with those of the others. Events have modified this grand design. Despite the Supreme Court's ruling in 1964 that each congressman must represent the same number of constituents, making the House even more egalitarian, it tends to be the less likely of the two chambers to disturb the *status quo*. The representatives are so intent on furthering the particularistic interests of their localities that they hardly have the time or inclination to forge broad national policy initiatives. Rather than acting the part of statesman, the representative is expected to 'do something' for the relatively small area (fewer than 500,000 persons) that elected him. Often the district has a single, dominant economic interest, such as wheat farming or steel manufacturers. A representative may measure his success by the amount of government money, in the form of defence contracts, public works and the like, that he can funnel home.

The Senate has not been affected by the reapportionment ruling because the constitution prohibits denying any state equal franchise in the Senate without its permission, a provision which is not subject to amendment. The only major alteration in the Senate has been the Seventeenth Amendment (1913), which provided for the election of Senators rather than appointment by the state legislatures. Alaska's 300,000 citizens thus enjoy equal representation with California's 20 million. Of the 100 senators, 52 are elected by a mere 15 per cent of the nation's population. In spite of its undemocratic composition, however, the Senate tends to be rather more liberal than the House partly because senators cannot help but be more sensitive to urban interests. Many members of the House represent totally rural districts, but every senator has at least one city in his state. The mixture of economic, social and ethnic interests in statewide constituencies spares the Senate from the particularism that pervades the House.

Reinforcing the senators' relatively broad outlook is the status of their chamber as the breeding ground of presidential hopefuls. Presidents Nixon, Johnson, Kennedy and Truman were all elevated from the Senate, and presidential candidates Muskie, McGovern, Jackson, Humphrey, McCarthy and Robert Kennedy ran while they were senators. At any given moment a number of senators harbour ambitions for the White House and seek a national constituency, carefully avoiding stigmatization as a narrow 'corn belt' politician or a 'one issue' candidate.

The senators have frequent opportunities, in fact, to act as a kind of presidential peer group, sharing with the chief executive several important constitutional responsibilities. Although he is the nation's spokesman in foreign affairs, the President can conclude treaties only with their advice and consent. That prerogative affords senators a strong voice in foreign policy decisions. Moreover, almost all presidential appointees, including cabinet officers and Supreme Court justices, must be confirmed by the Senate. A prudent President consults the senators in advance about their preferences. The custom of 'senatorial courtesy' requires the nomination of federal judges and prosecuting attorneys to be approved by the senators of the states where they are to serve, assuming that the President and the senators are of the same party. In practice, that often means that these senators are able to 'suggest' a nominee to the President.

Apart from its heterogeneous constituency and its broad presidential outlook, the Senate tends to be more liberal because it is less burdened by the weight of seniority and autocratic committee chairmen. Influence in the Senate is more personal, more a reflection of the respect earned from one's colleagues than the result of seniority. It could hardly be otherwise among such an elite band of seasoned politicians, many of whom have served for years as congressmen or governors of states. The system, prevailing in the House, whereby a representative accumulates power in proportion to his length of tenure, ill suits a legislative body whose 'freshmen' may already be political veterans and perhaps national figures. Even the relatively swift upward mobility of the Senate is too slow for some; one senator announced disgustedly in 1973 that he would not stand for election for a second term because 'by the time you get any power around here, you're ready to kick the bucket'.

The real power in the upper chamber, often referred to as the Gentlemen's Club, lies in an inner circle whose membership is informal and fluid; observers disagree on just who are the members of the circle at any moment. Generally speaking, the most influential senators will be those known as 'work horses' or 'inside men', as distinguished from the 'show horses' and 'outside men'. The former diligently tend the legislative vineyards, caring for mundane Senate business, while the latter are out campaigning for President. As in any organization, those who are present most of the time and devoting their full energies become more influential than part-time or absentee members.

Like any gentlemen's club, the Senate has certain rules of procedure but not enough to make life too tedious. While the 435 members of the House must adhere closely to a bulky rule book and a strict time limit for speaking, the 100 senators can afford a relatively relaxed procedure and unlimited debate. That has given rise to a peculiar parliamentary tactic, the 'filibuster', in which a minority opposed to a bill refuses to stop talking until the measure is withdrawn. If the bill's sponsors could not obtain a two thirds majority on a motion for 'cloture', they often had to drop their bill in order to allow the rest of the agenda to be considered. A filibuster is particularly effective when the Senate is under pressure to deal with a backlog of bills.

A time-honoured senatorial custom, filibustering has produced some colourful moments. Senator Huey Long of Louisiana, a legendary figure in American politics, spoke for $15\frac{1}{2}$ hours in 1935, punctuating his remarks with recipes for cooking chicken gumbo and other southern delicacies. In 1953, Senator Wayne Morse of Oregon set the record for a one-man filibuster: 22 hours and 26 minutes, part of which he spent reading names from a telephone directory. Stamina, rather than relevance, is the key to a successful filibuster.

Normally a group of senators will filibuster, yielding the floor to each other in turn. Opponents may try to stop the filibusterers from 'talking a bill to death' by seizing upon some parliamentary misstep to take the floor away or by forcing the Senate into continuous session, both sides sleeping on cots in the hallways to be ready for a sudden vote. Usually, however, a cloture motion is necessary, and that has succeeded only about two dozen times since 1917.

Although it seems like a quaint ritual, the filibuster was a powerful tool in the hands of southern senators, who were able to obstruct civil rights legislation for many years. Two major civil rights bills, the 1964 act prohibiting racial discrimination in places of public accommodation and the 1968 act outlawing discrimination in housing sales, were passed only after southern filibusters were narrowly beaten. In earlier attempts, the southerners were able to muster more than one third of the Senate to vote against cloture because some senators, although unsympathetic to the southern cause, were nevertheless devoted to the principle of unrestricted debate. Senators from small-population states argue that the right to filibuster makes their voice more important in the legislative process, helping to balance the influence of large states in the House. Even liberals at times have deigned to take advantage of unlimited debate to try to thwart legislation they opposed. The filibuster, in short, amounts to a *liberum veto*, a potential veto possessed by every member of the Senate, and none is eager to divest himself of it.

Nevertheless, the Senate did modify its rules in 1975 to reduce the required cloture majority from two thirds to three fifths, which should make it somewhat easier to halt a filibuster. The modification reflected growing appreciation of the wisdom of Senator Henry Cabot Lodge the Elder's remark that 'to vote without debating is perilous, but to debate and never vote is imbecile'.

Dilatory practices like the filibuster contribute to the sluggish performance which has earned Congress its poor reputation. Most of the contemporary proposals for reform of that institution are aimed at eliminating such archaic customs as well as displacing those power-brokers who can block legislation single-handed. The growing strength of the speaker-in-caucus bodes ill for the House committee barons, and there is a movement afoot to limit congressmen to a fixed number of terms to prevent personality cults from developing. Such structural changes are not a perfect substitute for well-disciplined parties, but they should at least inspire somewhat greater public confidence in the capacity of Congress to deal with the problems of the day.

6 The Supreme Court: Judicial Politics

Immediately after the 1970 congressional elections, *The Times* of London noted that proposals to lower the voting age were rejected by the voters in ten of the fifteen states where these proposals had been put to a referendum: 'The issue will be decided this term by the Supreme Court, which will almost certainly take the result of the state elections into account,' the report continued. To readers this may have appeared to be sociological jurisprudence carried to a ludicrous extreme or some primitive system of adjudication by popular acclamation. Of course, when the constitutionality of the federal statute fixing the voting age at eighteen was challenged in the court, the petitioners were not obliged to cite the election statistics in their brief, but the saying that the justices 'follow the election returns' is a maxim of American politics on which constitutional lawyers rely. What the maxim implies – something that foreign observers may misunderstand – is that the United States Supreme Court is not just a court, at least not in the usual sense of the word. To describe it merely as a court is to ignore the most important implications of its work, for it is very much a part of the political process.

The British jurist Lord Devlin has said that the English judicial mind 'hates politics'. But in the mind of the American Supreme Court justice, it is a daily consideration. The business of the court is often described as 'judicial politics', and probably almost as many political scientists as lawyers pore over its opinions. By constitutional pronouncements the court resolves many important issues of policy and brings others into public prominence. In recent decades, for example, the court has engendered such political *causes célèbres* as racial integration of schools, reapportionment of the legislatures, abolition of capital punishment and legalization of abortion.

The court, in fact, is expected to respond to broad changes in public opinion with new constitutional doctrines. That is why the justices are presumed to be analysing the voting results. That is also why the creative court, which had been headed for fifteen years by the late Chief Justice Warren, is being watched for signs of retreat. In their 1968 election campaigns, President Nixon and Governor George Wallace of Alabama struck a responsive chord in the American public by attacking the court for its liberalism, and the currently popular 'law and order' political campaigns usually denounce the justices for being overly solicitous of the rights of accused criminals.

The justices may take comfort, however, from the failure of Congress to exercise its constitutional authority to restrict the court's jurisdiction. Indeed, the Senate thought so highly of the court that it incurred the extreme displeasure of the President by rejecting two of Nixon's nominees for the bench, one because the nominee's honesty was suspect, the other because he was thought to be 'mediocre'. Even the severest critics seem ambivalent, anxious to withdraw power from the court with one hand and confer it with the other. Governor Wallace, a staunch opponent of what he considers judicial interference with state prerogatives, nevertheless did not hesitate to petition the court to override the officials of one state when they refused to list him on the 1968 presidential ballot.

Such ambivalence points to the court's fundamental weakness as an institution of government: the court suffers from a permanent crisis of identity that exposes it to periodic attacks on its authority by those who happen to disagree with its judgements. Popular disfavour has characterized much of the court's history. Accusing the court of coddling criminals, atheists and pornographers, today's conservative critics resemble the liberals of the 1930s, criticizing the 'Nine Old Men' who, with dismaying regularity, held unconstitutional the economic reform legislation of President Franklin D. Roosevelt's New Deal. The ideology of the critics has changed but not their method of attack. They invariably accuse the court of having overreached itself, of having exceeded its constitutional powers. There are many who disagree with the policies of the President or of Congress, but they do not nearly as often question the authority of those branches of government to act as they have. The accusation against the court is difficult to answer, because its Achilles' heel is that its constitutional authority is imperfectly defined and largely self-proclaimed.

One of America's distinctive contributions to the science of government was the addition of a third and co-equal branch, the judiciary, to the executive–legislative division of governmental powers. But it has never been entirely clear what role the framers of the constitution intended for their innovation. Article III of the constitution simply gives the court appellate jurisdiction to hear 'all cases in law and equity' arising under the constitution, laws and treaties of the United States – with such exceptions as Congress might wish to make. The article also provides for 'such inferior Courts as the Congress may from time to time ordain and establish'. The remainder of the federal court system was created by the Judiciary Act of 1789 and has been maintained ever since. However, Congress may, whenever it wishes, abolish every federal court except the Supreme Court, subject to the possible exception that it cannot use that power to deprive persons of their constitutional rights. Today there are ninety-four district courts, at least one in each state, and eleven courts of appeal, each having jurisdiction over a group of states. The Supreme Court hears cases on appeal from these courts and from the highest courts of the fifty state judicial systems.

The Federalist, arguing for ratification of the proposed constitution, assured citizens in 1788 that the judiciary would be the 'least dangerous' branch of the government because it had neither 'force nor will' but could only decide cases at law that were brought before it. The authors of those predictions may or may not have been surprised by Chief Justice Marshall's declaration in 1803 that the court had the power to declare acts of Congress unconstitutional. Whether the constitutional convention intended or expected the court to assume the power of judicial review of legislation is still a matter of dispute, since the question was never discussed by the delegates. Because of the historical ambiguity of its mission, the court has been left to carve its own sphere of influence by proclamations such as Marshall's. While often acting as arbiter between Congress and the President, between the states and the federal government, the court has had no one but itself to define its role. The result, inevitably, has been an appearance of arbitrariness in the court's actions.

That appearance has heightened the natural suspicions aroused by a court of permanent appointees in a government otherwise composed of temporary officials in the upper echelons. Justices are nominated by the President, confirmed by a majority vote of the Senate and serve '. . . during good Behaviour', which means for life unless impeached by Congress. Often viewed as an anomalous institution in a democracy, the court is peculiarly vulnerable to recrimination for having thwarted the will of the majority. That was the accusation when the conservative court was laying waste the New Deal reform programme, and that has been the accusation in recent years, when the court was decreeing change while the legislatures and executive officials, both state and federal, admonished it for going too far too fast.

A rigidly conservative court might have been anticipated originally, because lawyers are assumed by nature and training to be conservative. That usually prescient observer, de Tocqueville, predicted early in the nineteenth century that the legal profession and the judiciary would prove to be the only pillar of stability in the American democracy. The spectacle of a progressive judiciary, initiating change in the face of opposition by a conservative legislature, would not have escaped the sense of irony of the Frenchman nor of the founding fathers, whose fears of the unbridled popular will drove them to erect the elaborate system of 'checks and balances' primarily against legislative excesses.

Because unforeseen, the liberal activist court has not been explicitly limited by the constitution. A conservative court can be counter-balanced by a progressive legislature; statutes declared unconstitutional can be redrawn and may eventually survive through reincarnation. But when the court is initiating changes in the schools, in housing patterns and in legislatures themselves, there are remarkably few constitutional means of checking and balancing. The President cannot veto a court decision, and Congress cannot nullify it by statute. Apart from restricting the court's jurisdiction, a clumsy recourse, virtually the only method of reversing a decision is the difficult process of formally amending the constitution. Winning the approval of a two-thirds majority of both Houses of Congress and then of the legislatures of three quarters of the states is a feat that is out of the question in all but the rarest moments of political consensus. Thus it has been possible for the court as social and political reformer to range freely, rewriting the law of the land

In the process, the court has done much to bring about social and political equality. It has proven eagerly responsive to what Justice Oliver Wendell Holmes termed 'the felt necessities of the time', promulgating by judicial fiat racial equality in schools and in housing, equality of representation in the legislatures, and equality of the poor before the law. But the court has also made its position more precarious, because no branch of the government has less moral authority to be the prime mover of social change than a body of nine Platonic Guardians, insulated by lifetime tenure against the direct pressure of the electorate.

The consequences of emphasizing that contradiction eventually manifest themselves, for to declare the law is one thing, to enforce it quite another. Whether, for example, the court's 1968 prohibition of racial discrimination in house sales (*Jones v. Mayer*) does indeed transform the pattern of segregated housing in America largely depends on the willingness of citizens and the other organs of government to implement the judgement. Having no enforcement mechanism, the court's power is the power of public opinion. As Justice Felix Frankfurter observed: 'The Court's authority – possessed neither of the purse nor the sword – ultimately rests on sustained public confidence in its moral sanction.'

The ultimate popular defence against an unpopular decision is simply to ignore it. The practical result of the famous 1954 school desegregation decision, *Brown v. Board of Education*, demonstrated that the reservoir of public deference to the court is not inexhaustible. More than twenty years after *Brown*, half of the black students in the south still attend schools that are predominantly black, because implementation was left to recalcitrant local school authorities supported by community sentiment. Securing compliance was difficult enough when the court was dealing only with segregation mandated by the laws of the southern states. A vestige of the south's 'peculiar institution' of slavery, segregation was wrought by state law and presumably could therefore be abolished by legal processes. But when the court began to require integration of northern schools, it was dealing with segregation sustained by patterns of residential settlement. While these patterns were the product of discriminatory attitudes among whites, they were nevertheless demographic facts not easily erased by judicial decision. Ordering pupils bussed to schools outside their neighbourhoods has been the judiciary's primary method of forcing integration, but where it has been done it has often provoked intense popular opposition and violent resistance.

Apart from creating practical problems of enforcement when it undertakes to satisfy what it believes are 'felt necessities', the court often appears to be disregarding the separation of powers doctrine, which confers equal status on the legislative, executive and judicial branches of the federal government. The housing decision ignored the delicate compromises in the housing section of the Civil Rights Act of 1968, which had been passed by Congress a few weeks earlier. Although the act exempted certain types of dwellings, the judicial decision prohibited racial discrimination in the sale or rental of every dwelling in the country. The opinion of the court, to be sure, was more satisfying logically than the act. Yet the passage of an 'open-housing' statute had been considered a monumental political achievement. The court might have recognized that, deferred to Congress and achieved almost the same result. One justification advanced for the court's 'legislating' expansively is that there frequently occurs what has been called a 'deadlock of democracy'. For example, southerners, by virtue of seniority, may be occupying all the crucial congressional committee chairmanships and obstructing passage of civil rights legislation. But even assuming this to be a pathological political condition calling for judicial remedy, the emergence of the Civil Rights Act of 1968 indicated that the legislative processes were in fact working well.

Many critics, including dissenters on the court, have warned that the only barrier to the court's infringement of legislative prerogative is the justice's self-restraint. Whenever possible, they argue, an appointive court ought to defer to the judgement of a popularly elected legislature. But whether one is a proponent of 'judicial restraint' or 'judicial activism' usually turns upon whether one agrees with the court's current decisions. The difficulty in formulating a rule of restraint that would satisfy both liberals and conservatives is that the court often must choose among competing public policy alternatives. The choice merely masquerades as a case in constitutional law. As de Tocqueville noted, Americans are quick to take differences of opinion about what the government should do and reduce them to legal questions to be brought before a court. The problem, for example, of how to draw constituency boundaries for state legislatures may be reduced to a Fourteenth Amendment question of 'equal protection of the laws', but it also is a question of policy that traditionally has exercised the political parties of the states.

By invoking the doctrine of 'political questions', the court for a long time avoided proffered opportunities to try to settle such disputes over policy. Certain issues were considered not amenable to judicial resolution and were relegated to the political process, because although the court might decide the legal aspects, it could not easily provide a remedy. Justice Frankfurter, a political liberal, alluded to that difficulty when he cautioned his colleagues against holding that inequality of population among constituencies was a justiciable issue. Courts, he said, 'ought not to enter this political thicket'. The thicket he foresaw has become apparent to the many district court judges who have had to supervise the drawing of boundaries, or actually draw the lines themselves, ever since the court, in 1964, held that congressional (*Wesberry v. Sanders*) and state legislative (*Reynolds v. Sims*) constituencies must be equal in population. The judges have had to make the choices that had been so bitterly fought over by the politicians.

The Supreme Court itself was soon visited with the consequences of its reapportionment rulings. In subsequent cases it was called upon to decide whether the difference of a few percentage points in the population of constituencies, not a gross disparity, was constitutionally permissible. The phrase 'equal protection of the laws' afforded little guidance, but the court did not hesitate to hold that constituencies must be as near to mathematical equality as is humanly possible. Despite the fundamentalist tone of the decision it was, after all, an exercise of discretion that was difficult to disguise as a clear constitutional constraint.

Whatever the difficulties involved in abandoning the 'political questions' doctrine, it must be said that only the court could have rectified an injustice like disproportional representation; left to the political process, it never would have been corrected. Here is a genuine 'deadlock of democracy'. Legislators from rotten boroughs understandably resist voting themselves out of office by approving bills to create constituencies that are equal in population, and often those legislators have an unjustified stranglehold over the legislatures. If the rights of the 'under-represented' – in this case, the majority of voters – were ever to be vindicated, they had to be vindicated at the bar of the court. It was left to the 'undemocratic' court to make America more democratic.

The reapportionment cases were only the latest example of the Supreme Court's historic role as a court of last resort for citizens shunned by the popularly elected institutions of government. Ignored by Congress and the state legislatures since the 1870s, blacks waged a campaign of litigation before the court in this century that succeeded in striking down numerous racial restrictions and culminated in the school and housing decisions. Defendants in criminal cases, who are not likely to be regarded by an elected official as a significant pressure group, have had their chances of fair treatment vastly expanded by the court while the legislators were denouncing rising crime rates.

That blacks were disenfranchised in many states and that defendants in criminal cases formed no discernible voting bloc did not deter critics from excoriating the court as a usurper of congressional and state legislative prerogatives. When criticism of its decisions, however unjustified, becomes as intense as it has been in these instances, the court may have to gauge carefully how much further it may go without endangering its ability to command public acceptance. A former United States solicitor general, Archibald Cox, has posed the court's dilemma in this way: 'The question is, how much and how fast can a court pursue what it sees as the goals of society without impairing the long run usefulness of judge-made law in contributing to their achievement?' Since the court's effectiveness depends on popular recognition of its word as authoritative, the justices may have to strike a balance in the future between advancing social ideals and conserving judicial prestige. It is tempting, no doubt, for the court to opt for social justice; the gains are immediate and obvious. The losses to the court in the erosion of its authority are hidden until the accumulation of 'self-inflicted wounds' leaves the court critically weakened.

Why the American people believe that 'the constitution is what the judges say it is', not what the legislators say it is, remains an enigma. But at least part of the answer is the obviously great popular reverence of the 'higher law' embodied in the written constitution, which is regarded as immutable, above mere politics, and revealed by judicial hierophants. The justices have been accorded the position of keepers of the constitutional mysteries because they too are believed to be above politics in the way that a legislature, subject to regular elections, never can be. It has been aptly remarked, however, that the court is moving towards a 'legislative mode' of conducting its business. It exhibits that notorious legislative phenomenon, the pre-adjournment rush: judgement in many of the most sensitive cases is postponed until the approaching end of term in June increases the pressure for compromise. The numerous *amicus curiae* (friends of the court) briefs, which offer no novel legal arguments but do emphasize the large membership of the associations submitting them, have become a form of lobbying.

The most significant similarity, however, between the court and the legislature is that the justices often treat their previous decisions as cavalierly as the legislators do theirs. Depreciating *stare decisis*, the rule that legal precedents must be followed, can be especially dangerous for the court, making it seem politically expedient as well as confounding the popular notion of the immutability of the 'higher law'. Too sudden fluctuations of doctrine call into question the justices' subordination of mere personal preference to the supposedly timeless principles of the constitution, especially when doctrines only recently reaffirmed are overruled without decent mention by a 5-4 vote. Rather than seize the first opportunity to overrule a precedent in the name of social justice, the court might better bide its time until it had the authority of unanimity on the bench. However, that cannot be an inflexible rule. The *Brown* decision was unanimous but had there been only a 5-4 majority, it still would not have been preferable to let school segregation laws survive for another few decades in order to conserve the institutional authority of the court. The difficulty with *stare decisis*, like Christianity, is that it has never been practised, and anyone who begins practising it will be at a distinct disadvantage. The court paid little heed to *stare decisis* when it first approved of the segregationist 'separate but equal' doctrine in 1896, and it would have been unfair to demand of the justices who were considering *Brown* more respect for precedent than shown by their predecessors.

Whatever the merits of *stare decisis* as a legal principle, its political implications are conservative. To that extent, it conflicts with the burden that the court is increasingly called upon to assume: representing the unrepresented. These – the young, the black, the poor, the female, the criminally suspect, the politically dissident – all are demanding change. Although new personnel may give the bench a more conservative complexion, it will be difficult for the court to refuse entirely the sympathetic response that these petitioners have been led to expect.

As their champion, the court is doomed to unpopularity, because for the most part it will be opposing the majority. But the role is appropriate for at least two reasons. First, the unrepresented are those whom other branches of government have ignored, intentionally or unintentionally. Secondly, the essence of the entrenched rights in the constitution is the notion that there are some things which cannot be done to an individual or minority group even by majority vote; hence, the court, as chief interpreter of 'due process of law' and 'equal protection of the laws', will be acting simply as referee of democracy's rules of the game.

The first consideration recognizes that prudence requires avoiding bitter clashes over what other branches regard as their special preserves. For example, the court did not accomplish anything significant other than to conjure the spectre of an internecine confrontation with Congress, when it ruled the exclusion of a member of the House of Representatives by his colleagues unconstitutional in 1969. The issue was probably moot, since the legislative session had expired, and unlikely to arise again, yet the court handed down an opinion which greatly antagonized congressmen by presuming to judge their internal rules of organization.

The emphasis upon due process may seem to presage a revival of the now disgraced doctrine of 'substantive due process'. What made the Nine Old Men of the 1930s obsolete was their rigid application of this doctrine to government regulation of private economic activity. They would frequently construe the substance of an act as 'unreasonable', hence as a denial of due process, even though there were no irregularities of procedure. It is unfortunate that association with the *ancien régime* has stigmatized the idea that the substance of law, its effect as well as its ostensible procedural fairness, is worthy of consideration. Political scientists, after all, long ago abandoned the study of formal rules and procedures of organizations because they found themselves looking at the trees rather than the forest, and minority groups have realized from painful experience that procedural equality does not necessarily mean substantial equality of results.

The constitution, to be sure, is more than a charter of individual liberties, and it may be objected that the court has other tasks. However, many of the classic and recurrent controversies in which the court has taken part have been largely settled. The balance of power in the federal system has been thrown permanently to the national government; the power of Congress to regulate the economic life of the country has been firmly established. Except for refinements of doctrine, the court has relatively little left to say about such issues. There is, however, a great clamouring for individual and group liberties by those who have not been heard from before. To this issue, the court has a great deal to contribute, because it can determine the scope and meaning of 'due process' and 'equal protection'. Given the alternatives, most nations would consider themselves fortunate if the tensions and dissensions of their societies could be settled in court.

Whether the court sustains the progressive spirit of the Warren era, from 1953 to 1969, or humbly defers to the more 'democratic' branches of government hinges upon the justices whom the President nominates. The custom of referring to a 'Roosevelt Court' or a 'Nixon Court' reflects the enormous, if indirect, presidential influence on constitutional doctrine. Although tenured for life, justices die or voluntarily retire often enough to enable Presidents to choose successors about every two years. On the average, a President serving both four-year terms could thus expect to nominate almost a majority of the court.

By gracefully accommodating the immutable to the inevitable, fresh appointees have allowed the court to survive changes in the national consensus. Franklin D. Roosevelt's appointment of prominent New Dealers to the court ensured the judicial acceptance of his policies and saved the court from an ignominious last stand that could only have been fatal to its power as an institution. Many a justice, however, has surprised a President by changing his views dramatically after joining the bench. While a conservative governor of California, Earl Warren gave little hint of becoming a liberal chief justice, and President Eisenhower ruefully concluded that appointing him was 'the biggest damfool mistake I ever made'.

Probably, what emerges in new justices are opinions suppressed during either a political career of lipservice to parochial orthodoxies or a legal career whose professional arguments have been mistaken for personal views. More would be known about the judicial outlook of appointees were it not that remarkably few of them have ever been judges before. Even chief justices have been drawn mainly from non-judicial outsiders rather than sitting members of the bench. President Johnson's unsuccessful attempt to elevate Justice Abe Fortas to chief justice in 1968 illustrates the difficulties of promoting from within; any sitting justice acquires a certain infamy in the course of deciding controversial cases. In fact, to hold out the hope of being appointed chief is to encourage a justice to temper his opinions with an eye on the President and the Senate. The consequences for judicial independence are obvious.

Apart from being a lawyer–politician whose views are palatable to the President, an important advantage for an aspiring justice is to be a member of his party. All things being equal, Presidents prefer to award these most prestigious of patronage plums to loyal followers of the party he leads.

Although the Supreme Court was not intended to be a representative body, the notion that the court should mirror the nation politically, ethnically and geographically is well entrenched. To modify a rallying cry of the American Revolution, there can be 'No adjudication without representation'. When a vacancy occurs, it may be referred to as the 'Jewish seat' or the 'Catholic seat', or a President may pledge, as Nixon did, to give the southern states a 'voice' on the court. The emergence of ethnic groups in the political arena may be signalled by the appointment of a token justice. President Johnson nominated the first black justice at the height of the civil rights movement of the 1960s: the eventual nominations of a Spanish-speaking American, an Indian, and a woman can be safely anticipated. (A Spanish-speaking Indian woman would be the ideal candidate.)

The representative principle does contradict the juristic ideal of impartial decision by the rules of logic, but, as Holmes observed, the life of the law is experience, not logic. Uniquely among jurists, the Supreme Court justice is free to decide according to a sense of justice that is a product of his life experience. In the American context, that is a strength rather than a defect. It is a chief reason why, in the hands of the Supreme Court, the constitution has stayed a flexible, useful basis for political life, rather than the remote codification of outmoded ideas, imposing the dead hand of the past.

The very process by which the justices arrive at their collective decision emphasizes independence of mind rather than devotion to a neat abstraction called 'the law'. For decisions of the court are made by negotiation and compromise, not merely ratiocination. In practice, after oral arguments are heard in a number of cases, the justices meet in private conference to embark upon the tortuous path of decision. Speaking in order of reverse seniority on the bench, each justice explains his position. They debate the issues for a time, trying not so much to convert each other as to search out common ground. Unanimity is considered desirable, of course, but no attempt is made to pressure dissenting justices into standing shoulder to shoulder so as to present a monolithic front. Writing dissenting opinions is an old and honoured tradition. The dissent is considered an appeal to future generations, who in many cases have indeed found more wisdom in the dissenting opinions than in the majority's words. Some, like Holmes, have been as influential through their memorable dissents as through their opinions for the court.

After the discussion in conference, a vote is taken. The chief justice has only one vote, but as 'first among equals' enjoys the customary right to appoint the justice who will compose the majority opinion. If the chief is in the minority, the senior justice in the majority exercises that option. Sometimes a chief justice, realizing that he is of the minority view, votes the opposite of his conviction in order to place himself in a position to minimize the damage, either by writing the opinion himself or choosing the majority justice most sympathetic to his views. In that manner, the strength of the opinion may be diluted.

A draft opinion is then circulated, and dissenting opinions are composed. At this stage, too, justices may alter their views, or, in return for a concession by the opinion writer, change sides. Even when justices agree about the outcome, they frequently disagree about the reason for it, making it necessary to obscure or ignore some issues in the opinion in order to hold a majority together. That does not usually make for a very coherent or satisfying opinion. At times the court is riven with dissension, and the justices, 'concurring in part and dissenting in part', bring forth nine separate and mutually contradictory opinions. Determining what, if anything, such a decision really stands for is not an easy task for constitutional lawyers, much less the public.

In most cases, however, the court is not so splintered but rather exhibits a phenomenon known as bloc voting. Usually a conservative bloc and a liberal bloc exists, and sometimes one or two 'swing votes' who determine which of the blocs shall prevail in any given case. The solidarity of these blocs may vary from issue to issue but overall their cohesion can be statistically remarkable. In the 1973–4 term of the court, for example, the four justices appointed by President Nixon, forming a conservative bloc, voted together in 75 per cent of the cases. With a single exception, they succeeded in attracting at least one other justice in each case so as to form a majority.

The hegemony of one bloc or the other at various periods in the court's history is what makes for 'eras'. During the Warren era a bloc of at least five justices, including the chief, regularly voted together to produce its characteristic liberal jurisprudence. By the early 1970s, the liberal bloc had been diminished by attrition to three members, and dominance of the court passed to the bloc of Nixon justices. The transition was not marked by a sharp change of direction. While the new court has been noticeably less eager to expand the rights of criminal defendants any further, it has scaled some heights of judicial activism unattained even in the Warren era. In 1972, the court abolished the death penalty as commonly imposed and in the following year announced the constitutional right to an abortion. It has continued to apply the premises of the reapportionment decisions. In the field of civil rights, the court has broadened protections against discrimination in voting and employment but has been more reluctant to force school integration especially where segregation is caused by residential patterns. The new court, in general, has slowed the pace of liberal activism but has not conducted a *coup d'état* against the principles of the Warren era. The court has been more responsive to its own recent traditions than to the appointing authority.

Besides personnel changes, the Supreme Court faces the possibility of a reorganization of the structure of the appellate judicial system in the near future, a step which could have far-reaching consequences. Proposals for the reorganization have arisen, in judicial circles and elsewhere, because of the enormous increase in recent decades of the court's caseload. In 1951, only about 200 cases were filed annually; by 1975 the number had exceeded 5000. Since the Supreme Court need accept only the cases it wishes to review – in those not reviewed the lower court ruling is left standing – the overwhelming majority of the cases filed are denied a hearing. The justices hear and decide only about 150 cases a year. However, the effort required merely to screen out the other cases imposes a crushing burden on the nine justices, who must at least cursorily read the preliminary briefs. Unlike the other branches of government, the court is in no position to rely upon expanded staff to cope with its burgeoning workload; each justice has but two law clerks to assist him. Moreover, many cases are denied review simply because the justices must ration their time, not because the suits lack intrinsic importance. In some instances, the failure to review a case leaves standing conflicts among decisions of the courts of appeals.

Three main proposals have been put forward for dealing with the caseload, all of them suggesting the interposition of another court between the Supreme Court and the existing lower courts. One proposal is to create a court that would perform the screening, handing up to the Supreme Court only those it deemed most important. This proposal has met with the objection, that it would abridge the right of litigants to have access to the Supreme Court. A second proposal would assign whole categories of cases such as tax law, to the new court; agreement has been lacking, however, about which categories to treat in this manner. A third plan would have the Supreme Court accept its usual 150 cases but assign another 150, which would otherwise go undecided, to the new court. The principal defect of this plan is that the Supreme Court might ultimately need to review the decisions of the new court as well. Thus, a new court would have been added to the judicial hierarchy without decreasing the burden on the Supreme Court. Whatever alternative is adopted, the difficulty of finding an acceptable substitute for the personal attention of the Supreme Court is a touching indication of popular faith in that institution.

7 The Bureaucracy: Administrative Politics

Most bureaucratic tables of organization appear simple on paper and complex in reality; the American bureaucracy is complex even on paper. For although the executive branch is divided along functional lines into eleven main departments, the equivalent of British ministries, alongside them exist more than forty independent commissions, boards, agencies, administrations, corporations, foundations, institutions, authorities, systems and services. Another two dozen agencies form a kind of super-cabinet level within the Executive Office of the President, the apex of the bureaucratic pyramid. In so ponderous an apparatus, it is hardly surprising that functions tend to overlap and that lines of authority are often blurred. The bureaucracy departs from the rational model because the executive branch was not created according to plan but was built up, like a coral reef, by accretion. Each agency represents an attempted solution to a problem at some time in the nation's history. Much of the confusion and overlap betokens the ease of creating new agencies compared with abolishing old ones.

The framers ignored the subject of administrative organization. The constitution mentions the 'executive departments' only in passing, by stipulating that the President 'may require the opinion, in writing, of the principal officer in each'. It was left to Congress to create the departments by statute as it saw fit. Today there are, in order of seniority, Departments of State (foreign relations); Treasury; Defense; Justice; Interior; Agriculture; Commerce; Labor; Health, Education and Welfare; Housing and Urban Development; and Transportation. The first two departments were established in the late eighteenth century, the last two in the 1960s.

The secretaries who head each of these departments are appointed by the President, with the consent of the Senate, and constitute his cabinet. Secretaries are not sitting members of the legislature nor are they responsible to it. The extent to which the cabinet exists at all as a decision-making body varies with the preferences of the President. Eisenhower frequently called upon the cabinet to make decisions collectively; Johnson sought the 'consensus' of cabinet thinking while reserving decisions for himself; Nixon convened his cabinet infrequently and favoured the advice of the White House staff.

Except for the secretary of state, whose chief duties are diplomatic, the cabinet members are primarily administrators. Their authority is exercised not collectively, in council, but severally as the overseers of the executive departments. Relying upon these departments to implement legislation, Congress has delegated to them considerable discretion. About 100 agencies are empowered to issue rules, regulations and orders which, when printed in the *Federal Register*, the official gazette, have the force of statute. Administrators' faithfulness to their legislative mandate is kept under constant review by Congress, which approves departmental budget requests, and they may be called to account by the courts. But the departments are surrounded by an aura of expertise to which the other branches defer, and between the poles of legislative and judicial scrutiny administrators enjoy wide latitude.

Perhaps the most severe restriction upon administrators is the structure of the bureaucracy, which does not necessarily correspond with the dimensions of its tasks. The urban crisis, for example, is a combination of unemployment, crime, welfare dependency, inadequate housing, and paralysing traffic congestion. Yet each of these aspects of the same problem falls under the jurisdiction of a different department, and co-ordination is often lacking. Even a relatively small objective, such as preserving a forest, can fall foul of bureaucratic divisions. One grove of the trees in the forest may be classified as 'National Park', the province of the Interior Department, while another is listed as 'National Forest', the province of the Agriculture Department. National parks are exclusively for conservation and recreation but one purpose of a national forest is to assure a supply of trees for lumbering. Securing agreement between the two departments, each with its own sets of rules and organizational interests, may prove difficult.

Even within the same department, there may be intense rivalries between subordinate bureaux whose 'missions' are in conflict. The Interior Department harnesses together two such agencies: the Bureau of Land Management and the Fish and Wildlife Service. Both are concerned with administration of the vast government lands, which lie mainly in the west, but their objectives are radically different. The Wildlife Service is concerned with preserving the game on public lands, but the BLM has been traditionally inclined to protect the rights of those who wish to graze livestock there or extract mineral deposits. Locked in perpetual warfare with each other, the two agencies strive to make their own goals prevail, each finding support in different 'constituencies'. The BLM expects the grazers' and miners' lobbies to do their bit on Capitol Hill, and the Wildlife Service relies upon the support of the conservationist groups. The shape of public lands policy will thus be determined by the outcome of an intra-mural struggle waged with the support of extra-mural political allies.

At times the departments appear to be mere holding companies for a collection of self-motivated bureaux, each with its own interest-group constituency and champions in Congress. Such units as the Federal Bureau of Investigation in the Justice Department and the Forest Service in the Agriculture Department have enough political support to make it difficult for the departmental secretaries to order them to do anything they are unwilling to do. Bureaux, moreover, like the FBI, have managed to establish their own 'closed-career' cadres which are removed from the regular civil service channels. New members are recruited directly after university graduation and spend their entire working lives within a single bureau, dependent upon the senior ranks for their promotions.

The bureau does not exchange personnel with other government offices. All members of the bureau may share a common professional background, such as lawyer, engineer, or geologist. As Herbert Kaufman has said of the Forest Service Officers, 'They are absorbed into the organization by a kind of gradual social osmosis, during which they, in turn, absorb many of the prevailing values, assumptions, and customary modes of operation.'

The autonomy of the bureaux leaves power in the executive branch diffused among many centres of decision-making. But while the independence of these bureaux is only informal, the class of 'independent agencies' is formally separated from the departments. The independent agencies have but one common characteristic: they are outside the control of the cabinet secretaries. Otherwise, they fall into two categories, those run by administrators directly responsible to the President and those which are headed by autonomous boards of commissioners serving fixed terms. The two categories have diametrically opposed purposes. The former allow the President to supervise certain government activities closely, while the latter take supervision of other activities entirely out of his hands.

The autonomous commissions were created to administer a variety of matters which, for one reason or another, Congress was reluctant to entrust to the regular departments or the President. Usually, the motive was to take politics out of the administrative process by employing bi-partisan boards one step removed from the chief executive's direct authority and patronage powers. Although the President, with the consent of the Senate, appoints the commissioners, they serve fixed terms and cannot be removed by him like ordinary administrators, except in clear cases of neglect of duty or malfeasance, as provided by statute. Since the commissioners' terms are longer than a presidential term (some are as long as fourteen years), any one President is unlikely to alter the composition of the board dramatically. Security of tenure assures the commissioners broad freedom.

Some commissions, such as the United States Postal Service and the Tennessee Valley Authority (which operates hydro-electric generating plants), are really public corporations functioning in a manner similar to private enterprises. Others, like the National Science Foundation and the National Foundation on the Arts and Humanities, operate like private charitable institutions, bestowing grants to support scientific, educational and cultural activities. But the most important group of commissions are those which exercise economic regulatory powers.

Beginning in the late nineteenth century, Congress created a number of agencies to control abuses in what had been until then essentially a *laissez-faire* economy. The first of these was the Interstate Commerce Commission, established in 1887 to set maximum rates for rail freight. In 1914, the Federal Trade Commission was created to control the monopolistic practices of the giant corporations, the 'trusts'. As part of President Roosevelt's New Deal of the 1930s, a number of other 'alphabet agencies' came into being, including the National Labor Relations Board, the Securities and Exchange Commission, and the Federal Communications Commission.

From the beginning, the regulatory commissions encountered the objection that Congress had unconstitutionally delegated its legislative powers to administrators in violation of the principle of separation of powers. For, while the statutes creating the commissions set down the basic policies to be followed, much discretion was left to administrators to make specific rules. The Federal Trade Commission for example, was charged with controlling 'unfair', that is, restrictive or monopolistic, trade practices, but it had to decide specifically which practices were to be labelled 'unfair'. By the early twentieth century the Supreme Court had accepted the necessity of at least some delegation of rule-making authority to administrators in order that the will of Congress be given practical effect. In distinguishing between constitutional and unconstitutional delegations of authority, the court has insisted only that sufficiently clear and specific standards be prescribed to guide the administrators' discretion. The court has even upheld the delegation to administrators of the power to make rules whose violation is a criminal offence.

Besides possessing quasi-legislative powers, the commissions exercise quasi-judicial functions. They decide when their rules have been broken, and they may enforce their judgements by issuing 'cease and desist' orders or by assessing fines. This, too, has brought complaints that functions properly committed to another branch of government have been usurped. In response, Congress has taken steps to make administrative proceedings more akin to those of courts in their respect for individual rights. It passed the Administrative Procedures Act in 1946, laying down uniform rules to preclude arbitrary decisions by administrators. Beyond that, however, the Supreme Court has held the commissions accountable to the Fifth Amendment's command that no person be deprived of life, liberty or property without due process of law. The most basic element of due process is the right to adequate notice and a hearing before the commission at which an individual affected by a proposed administrative action may enter his objections. As the Supreme Court declared in 1937, 'Those who are brought into contest with the government in a quasi-judicial proceeding aimed at the control of their activities are entitled to be fairly advised of what the government proposes and to be heard upon its proposals before it issues its final command.'

In the second category of independent agencies, those whose chiefs report directly to the President, are about a dozen units, including the Veterans Administration, the Environmental Protection Agency and the Federal Energy Administration. No imperative of logic requires them to be separated from the regular departments; the Veterans Administration, certainly, could be suitably sheltered under the umbrella of either the Defense Department or the Health, Education and Welfare Department. The creation of the energy and environmental agencies, both in the early 1970s, suggests that the main motivation is to establish highly 'visible' offices to deal with controversial issues. Merely creating a division within an existing department might give the impression that the problem was being buried, which is one indication of the degree of popular confidence in the regular bureaucracy.

Similar reasons explain the enormous proliferation, during the 1960s and 1970s, of agencies within the executive office of the President. Although the executive office once comprised only the closest staff advisers of the President, it has been filled out with agencies having direct administrative responsibilities. Some of these agencies, like the Domestic Council and the National Security Council, co-ordinate at a 'super cabinet' level matters falling within the jurisdiction of two or more departments, assuring co-ordination and suppressing inter-departmental feuds. In some instances, an agency can thoroughly dominate the departments it is supposedly 'co-ordinating'. Before officially assuming the title of Secretary of State, Henry Kissinger effectively supplanted the State Department while serving as director of the National Security Council. Other agencies, such as President Johnson's Office of Economic Opportunity, created to wage the war on poverty, were intended to administer new, high-priority programmes which the President feared to entrust to the more fossilized sections of the bureaucracy.

Probably the most powerful of the executive office agencies is the Office of Management and Budget. A descendant of the old Bureau of the Budget in the Treasury Department, the OMB was moved into the White House during the 1960s to give the President more control over his subordinates by applying the budget sanction systematically. The OMB has evolved into a general planning agency, reviewing departmental budget requests in the light of the President's overall strategy. By controlling the funds that each department gets, the OMB sets policy guidelines, determining which programmes shall be expanded and which run on thin rations. President Nixon relied heavily upon the budget agency to make the bureaucracy more responsive to him. Like other Presidents, Nixon some times found it exceedingly difficult to prod the lumbering apparatus into motion.

In its bulk, if not in its efficiency, the bureaucracy is an awe-inspiring sight. The federal government employs about three million civilians, and their occupations are almost as varied as those in the private sector. There are about 15,000 job categories, ranging from astronauts to specialists in chicken diseases. Half of the employees are engaged in defence-related activities, one quarter are in the postal service and the remaining one quarter are left to cope with all the rest: social services, housing, education, agriculture, conservation, law enforcement, commerce, labour and regulatory activities.

Those in the career civil service are expected to take vows of abstinence from politics. The Hatch Acts of 1939 and 1940 prohibit federal civil servants from taking 'any active part in political management or in political campaigns'. The acts were intended to prevent civil servants from being pressed into political service by their appointive bosses, but there are many who question the wisdom – or the constitutionality – of depriving so many of the citizen's right to participate in politics.

Civil servants have also been deprived of normal rights to unionize and bargain collectively over salaries and conditions of employment. By executive order, President Kennedy granted federal employees a limited right to bargain, but striking is still a felony. In most places in the United States, a strike by employees of any level of government – local, state, or federal – is regarded as a form of mutiny against lawfully constituted authority.

When paranoia over communist subversion was at its height in the 1940s and early 1950s, civil servants became particularly suspect. 'Loyalty boards' were created in most federal agencies to examine the political beliefs of thousands of civil servants, many of whom had been denounced by anonymous informers. A number of civil servants were discharged or resigned because their careers had been ruined by these witch hunts. The courts eventually blunted the sharper edges of the loyalty programmes by requiring procedural due process at the hearings and by limiting inquiries to civil servants in 'sensitive' positions.

From the way in which government employees are restricted and sometimes hounded, one may detect that the notion of a permanent civil service is still suspect. During the republic's first century, recruitment to government posts was conducted according to the principle that to the victor in politics belong the spoils of office. When a new President, especially of a party different from his predecessor's, entered the White House, there was virtually a complete turnover of officeholders. All but the clerical staff were replaced by political supporters of the new administration, and in some offices even the clerks were not spared.

There were, of course, arguments for the spoils system other than avarice. Among them was that 'sweeping Washington clean' every few years administered a strong antidote to corruption and entrenched power. Replacing officeholders frequently, it was contended, preserved democracy by preventing a mandarin class from forming and by affording a great number of citizens the opportunity to perform public duties. These duties were held to be simple enough for the average, reasonably intelligent person, regardless of his formal education. In the late nineteenth century, Professor Richard Hofstadter points out, 'The professional politicians succeeded in persuading themselves that civil-service reform . . . would restrict job-holding to a hereditary, college-educated aristocracy; and that all kinds of unreasonable and esoteric questions would be asked on civil service examinations.' Probably the most compelling reason for the spoils system, however, was that it provided a huge bonanza of patronage jobs, the promise of which candidates could use to induce party members to work for their election.

By 1883 Congress had tired of the excesses of amateurism and passed the Pendleton Act, which replaced the spoils system with the merit system for about three quarters of all federal posts. A civil service commission began to administer competitive examinations. The merit system gradually expanded until it covered about 90 per cent of all posts, but the large number of policy-making positions immediately under the cabinet secretaries are still filled mainly on partisan political grounds. Few career civil servants ever rise to positions equivalent to Permanent, Deputy or Under Secretary in Britain.

A change of administration still occasions a boom in the real estate market around Washington as incumbents prepare to leave for their home states and new appointees arrive. The period of uncertainty lasts for half a year or more, from election day in early November until several months after the new President takes office on 20 January. During this prolonged 'lame duck' period, the executive branch is not notably productive, since most of its important officials are either nervously contemplating the future or actively looking for another job. It is an exciting time for the Washington press corps, however, which avidly reports the names of those 'mentioned' for various posts.

The changeover is particularly thorough if one party has been in power for a long time. When Eisenhower assumed office in 1953, Republicans, who had been shut out of the sweepstakes for twenty years, were not only hungering for the usual appointive posts but demanding removal of many career civil servants who had risen through the ranks during the Democratic reign. The merit system by that time was well enough established to prevent the Republicans from completely satisfying their appetite for office, but many high-ranking civil servants who had become identified with Democratic policies were displaced.

Because of this system of recruitment, the upper echelons of the executive branch lack the continuity and professionalism of the British higher civil service. Most of the executive officials are businessmen, lawyers, academics or state politicians who have taken two or three years off from their regular occupations. While some have experience in private life which specifically equips them for their official tasks – a banker may become a Treasury Department official – many do not. According to the rules of campaign patronage, the talented and untalented alike must be given their just rewards. One reason why the bureaucracy tends to expand is the necessity to create non-critical posts which can be safely entrusted to the President's eager but less able political supporters. The Foreign Service offers a particularly good example of the patronage system in action; small African countries sometimes have been parcelled out *pro rata* to aspiring ambassadors according to the size of their campaign contributions.

Even when they are not incompetent, those who obtain positions through politics are likely to go on placing politics above official duty. At any given time, a number of federal bureaucrats may be planning to use their posts as stepping stones to elective offices, perhaps in their home states, so that political considerations weigh heavily with them. That is not immoral or illegal, but when the Assistant Secretary of Agriculture for International Affairs has his eye on the governorship of Iowa, it may be unclear whether his policy decisions are based on international conditions or conditions in Iowa

A similar doubt surrounds the official whose public service is merely an interlude in a business career. However honestly he endeavours to carry out his responsibilities, he can hardly keep from being influenced by his past and more especially his future. Can a person who has been an executive of a mining company, and intends to be one again, really take a detached view while serving as an official of the Bureau of Mines? Although interchange of personnel between government and industry is often considered an excellent way of bringing the hard-headed experience of businessmen into public service, the business world does not seem to do badly by the arrangement either.

In the field of defence, the ready exchange of personnel between government agencies and military contractors causes a certain blurring of distinctions which prompted President Eisenhower to warn against the growing influence of a 'military-industrial complex'. The Defense Department today buys vast quantities of goods and services from contractors. A congressional inquiry in the 1960s discovered that the 100 largest of these firms retained in their executive ranks 1400 former military officers, including 261 retired generals and admirals. The firm awarded the most contracts employed 187 former officers *and* a former Secretary of the Army. All of these ex-warriors obviously knew their way through the labyrinth of power in the Pentagon, where many of the civilian officials, too, are once-and-future employees of the contractors.

Some government departments, of course, exist primarily to promote the interests of private industry. The Departments of Agriculture, Commerce and Labor try to discover what their 'clientele' want done, so that government may do it for them. A famous case in point was the attempt by the Kennedy Administration to impose more stringent controls on farmers to reduce over-production of wheat; before it could legally do so, it was necessary for the Agriculture Department to put the question to a referendum of wheat farmers, who naturally voted against being regulated more strictly. The devolution of public power to officially recognized private interests is not always so glaring. But at all times, the representatives of interest groups are quietly making their wishes known to receptive administrators in the appropriate departments as well as to congressional committees.

In the business-oriented departments, the client relationship is quite open and recognized. But, unfortunately, even in those agencies whose ostensible mission is to regulate industry, not promote it, a covert client relationship often develops. The regulators become the captives of the regulated. The Interstate Commerce Commission, the oldest of the regulatory agencies, has set the pattern. Created in response to the railroads' exploitation of farmers who shipped grain, the commission was supposed to be a watchdog, curbing abusive practices by the rail companies. But today the commission is the railroads' chief protector. It allocates routes and sets rates in such a way as to guarantee them a generous profit in a safe, non-competitive environment. Ironically, the regulatory agencies that were supposed to eliminate restrictive business practices have elevated them to the status of government policy.

The capture of the regulatory agencies began with the practice of appointing commissioners with 'expertise', that is, in the case of the ICC, former railroad executives. Although the practice is natural in the client-centred departments, choosing regulators from among the regulated has proved self-defeating. Industry well understands this. When the Federal Energy Administration was being created in 1973, one large oil company paid a huge bonus to an executive who left to take a post in the new agency. Although a controversy erupted when the farewell gift was discovered, the assumption that oil executives without dowries are suitable for regulatory posts went unchallenged.

Even officials who were never business executives tend to develop undue sympathy for industry because of what has been delicately termed 'excessive interaction' between them and the businessmen they are supposed to regulate. An ICC member spends his working days – and sometimes his weekends – listening to the complaints of railroad executives, but he hardly ever has a conversation with a passenger. At formal hearings, moreover, all too often only the voice of industry is heard. To right the balance, a Consumer Advocacy Agency has been proposed that would have no administrative powers of its own but would represent consumer interests in regulatory agency proceedings. A bill to establish the consumer agency has failed in Congress several times, partly because of heavy lobbying by industry – an indication of how deeply it cherishes its exclusive 'interaction' with the regulators.

The regulatory agencies, however, are beginning to feel pressure from the 'public interest' organizations that represent non-industry views. By pressing their arguments at hearings and in the news media, these groups have started to force policy-making out into the open. Some notable victories have been won.

In 1974, the Federal Communications Commission decided for the first time not to renew the licence of a television station because of a complaint by a group of viewers about the station's performance. In previous years, broadcasters' applications had usually gone uncontested and were granted perfunctorily. Such counter-pressure may not be able to abolish entirely the cosy relationship between business and regulatory agencies, but it should at least dispel the myth of dispassionate administration and foster a frank recognition that the agencies are as much an arena of politics as is Congress.

8 Mass Media: The Fourth Branch

Two theories have been put forward to explain the role that the press plays in the American democratic system, each of them tied to widely divergent notions of how that system works. The traditional, and probably still most accepted, theory is that the press informs the sovereign electorate of what their officials are doing or planning to do, enabling 'public opinion' to crystallize. The press then takes soundings of public opinion and reports on the 'mood of the people' so that officials may make an appropriate response to the wishes of their constituents. This two-way theory assumes that citizens are rational beings, who gather facts and develop opinions about public affairs, and that officials pay attention to those opinions, as articulated by the press. It evokes a populist image of democracy, a town meeting writ large, in which the dialogue between officials and the electorate is carried on through the medium of the press. As Walter Lippmann, one of the most eminent American journalists, observed, 'Acting upon everybody for thirty minutes in twenty-four hours, the press is asked to create a mystical force called Public Opinion that will take up the slack in public institutions.'

The populist theory has enjoyed long currency. Although the early-nineteenth-century American press was coarse, abusive and violent in tone, de Tocqueville found 'it makes political life circulate in every corner of that vast land. Its eyes are never shut, and it lays bare the secret shifts of politics, forcing public figures in turn to appear before the tribunal of opinion.' Later in the century, Lord Bryce noted that 'in America public opinion is a power not satisfied with choosing executive and legislative agents at certain intervals, but [is] continuously watching and guiding those agents . . . The efficiency of the organs of opinion is therefore more essential to the government of the United States than even to England and France.'

Wholeheartedly embracing this view of its role, the press considers itself the adversary of government. Its job is to serve, as one modern American journalist has put it, as 'surrogate sovereign', a watchdog on behalf of the absent electorate. The newsman's mission is to ferret out corruption, malfeasance and misuse of the taxpayer's dollar. Without him, the newsman believes, the government would soon degenerate into an irresponsible cabal, perpetrating its schemes in secret.

There is, of course, a great deal of truth to that belief. Many government policies and plans die when exposed to the cruel light of day, which may prove that they were not fit to live in the first place. There are also deficiencies in the performance of government that would not be remedied were they not publicized. During the war in Vietnam, correspondents on the battlefields consistently deflated the false optimism of the Pentagon by sending home accounts which contradicted official assessments of the fighting. The press eventually moulded a popular consensus against continuing the conflict.

The second and more *avant-garde* theory of the press postulates an elitist form of democracy, in which officials pay lip service to the electorate while acting according to their own values and perceptions. Officials consult with each other rather than with the populace. The press reports information provided by officials mainly for the edification of other officials, thereby serving as a forum for those who make decisions.

The elitist theory portrays journalists as carrier pigeons rather than watchdogs. Their mission is not maintaining vigilance for the electorate but dispensing facts useful to officialdom. Proponents of the elitist theory point out that the American press has always had a peculiarly close working relationship with officials. Compared with those in many other countries, American officials go out of their way to feed the press information. They maintain 'press rooms' and retain public relations officers to deliver briefings as often as several times a day. Care is taken to meet the various deadlines of morning and afternoon newspapers. The press releases that are churned out diligently in Washington assure that reporters will always have a story. Informally, officials provide newsmen with juicy titbits at 'background briefings' or in the form of 'leaks', which the reporters cryptically attribute to 'usually reliable sources' and 'high government officials' so as to protect the informant's identity. (Reporters who have worked in Washington and London testify to the relative openness of American officials.) That the press observes these conventions is one measure of its dependence on the government information machine for satisfying its appetite for news.

The willingness of officials to supply information is not entirely altruistic. Officials use the press to promote their own goals and discomfit their enemies. Journalists may try to avoid being manipulated, but they do not really care about the motives behind a 'leak' so long as the information is accurate, which it usually is. Manipulation occurs in a variety of ways. Let us say that the President is planning to nominate a justice of the Supreme Court but is uncertain how the nomination will be received in the Senate, which must confirm the selection. He may try sending up a trial balloon by leaking to reporters the name of the person 'under serious consideration'. If a group of senators wished to discredit the nominee, it might then leak word that he was a bigamist or favoured vivisection. Embarrassed, the President might turn to another nominee. Thus, the entire confirmation debate would have been carried out in the press through leaks and counter-leaks.

In such cases, the elitist theory of the press seems quite accurate, for the newspapers merely serve as passive conduits for information voluntarily supplied by one set of officials to another set of officials. It is difficult to discern what role the electorate might play other than that of a Greek chorus. The elitist model is also supported by the fact, readily admitted by journalists, that the *Washington Post* has more influence upon the course of national events than does, for example, the *New York Post*. While that superior influence may be attributed to the quality of the former's staff, it is surely helped immeasurably by the newspaper's appearance upon the breakfast tables of all decision-makers in the capital. As a veteran of the Washington press corps has observed, 'Even if an official doesn't read it, his wife does and he hears all about it from her.' The *New York Post*, in contrast, may be read by the representatives and senators from New York as part of their office routine, but that would be the extent of its impact in Washington.

It may also be argued, in favour of the elitist model, that members of the press are themselves closer in opinions, attitudes, values and backgrounds to government officials than they are to the masses. How then can they pretend to serve as tribunes of the common people? The press, it is often claimed, is dominated by an 'Eastern Establishment' which reflects the concerns of politically liberal, educated persons living in big cities on the Atlantic seaboard but not those of the 'middle Americans' (i.e. middle class, midwestern and middle of the road) whose guardians they have appointed themselves. Thus, the policies that the press is likely to treat harshly and try to 'expose' may, in fact, be policies which most of the electorate endorses or is blissfully unconcerned about. When the press, at its hard-nosed best, tries to extort the truth from an official it suspects of malfeasance, most people may feel that the poor fellow is being unjustly persecuted. (Some persons, apparently, will forever believe that President Nixon was hounded out of office by the newspapers.) Consider the example of the FBI. The agency is normally discussed in ominous tones by the press because it is secretive and believed by many journalists to contain the germ of a Gestapo. Yet since most citizens are terrified by rising crime rates, they no doubt look gratefully upon the FBI as a bulwark against crime. Such discrepancies between popular sentiments and the professional biases of journalists produce a credibility gap between writer and reader. Survey evidence indicates that a vast number of people do not believe what they read in the papers or do not bother to read them at all.

Ironically for the watchdog theory, the press seems to be

believed more often by the officials it is supposed to be watching than by the populace whose interests it is supposed to protect. For while the public may be sceptical about what it reads in the papers, policy-makers depend on the media to bring problems to their attention. Officials were not blind to poverty, hunger, discrimination or opposition to the Vietnam War, but somehow they did not respond to them until the press made them real by documenting their existence. Minor social and economic dysfunctions, especially those confined to one state or region, often would not be noticed by Washington were they not discovered by the news media. The press thus helps set the agenda for government. A cruel prison system in Arkansas, discontent among the Indian tribes in Wisconsin, severe unemployment in Alaska – situations like these suddenly become important in the capital because the press makes them immediate. One merely has to count the number of references to newspaper articles in congressional debates to realize how heavily the legislators rely on the press as an intelligence network. Groups of the discontented have learned that lesson so well that the real purpose of most demonstrations and picket lines is to be a 'media event', that is to attract decision-makers' attention by getting into the papers or on television, thereby legitimizing their grievances. (Even dissidents overseas recognize the importance of carrying picket signs intelligible to an English-speaking television audience.) In recent years, the press has gained a better understanding of how its presence stimulates its subjects to perform. Television crewmen especially have learned to be less obtrusive at demonstrations.

The true function of the press probably lies somewhere between the elitist and the populist models. One might say it performs both functions simultaneously. In any day's issue of a newspaper, some of the stories will disclose information embarrassing to officials, retrieved from the darker recesses of government. Other stories will reveal information, like crime statistics and balance of trade figures, which the press probably could not have obtained had not the government compiled and released the data and answered questions at a briefing. The press would be poorer without both kinds of stories.

The balance between the inquisitive and disseminative roles of journalists has shifted somewhat towards the former since the Watergate affair of 1972–4, which was a crisis for the press as well as for the constitutional system. In many respects, Watergate represented American newsmen's finest hour. Displaying exemplary courage and initiative in reporting malefaction at the highest levels of government, the press stirred a lethargic Congress and judiciary to question seriously the probity of a President. Of all institutions, the press emerged from the scandal with the most enhanced reputation.

But Watergate also necessitated a sober re-evaluation of the customary ways of purveying information provided by government. Newsmen had suffered a betrayal and a loss of innocence. Throughout Watergate, many of those 'reliable sources' had proven amazingly unreliable, leaking erroneous tips, and many an official had looked reporters in the eye and blatantly dissembled. Gone was the traditional assumption that officials, though prone to embellish and self-serve, did not deliberately lie. As Katharine Graham, publisher of the *Washington Post*, commented: 'the process of deception has always been at least a theoretical possibility to working journalists throughout history. But in our time it became a major hazard.' The process of deception had first been detected during the Vietnam war in wildly exaggerated enemy 'body counts' and annual predictions of victory by Christmas. Yet those untruths were never so patent as in Watergate and did not involve moral turpitude or conspiracies to obstruct justice.

Concluding from Watergate that government was rife with corruption, many reporters embarked upon crusades to uncover it. 'Investigative reporting', blending the skills of the journalist and the private detective, became the watchword. Any official who had ever taken a shady political contribution or perpetrated a 'dirty trick' against an election opponent was liable to be exposed by hard-digging newsmen. Little Watergates were cropping up in the remotest villages. President

Nixon, after all, had proclaimed 'I am not a crook,' and it turned out that he had been lying. Why believe lesser officials when they said the same thing?

In its zeal, however, the press began to establish a single criterion by which to test an official's qualification for public office – honesty. It acted as if there were no germane questions to be asked about the suitability of a public official other than whether he was a criminal or a liar. In the rush to test the candour of those in public life, the press often neglected their opinions about public issues and their performance in previous offices. An example of this occurred during the congressional hearings in 1974 on the nomination of Nelson Rockefeller to be Vice President. Although he had been governor of New York for about fifteen years, the press hardly discussed his record in that office, preferring to concentrate on the ethics of his having made secret loans to other public officials.

The tone of hostility towards officialdom which some reporters have adopted may be straining the adversary relationship to the breaking point. By acting upon the premise as one reporter put it, that 'there is only one way for a newsman to look at politicians, and that is down', the press could jeopardize its traditional close ties to government. What is gained by subjecting officials to trial by ordeal may be lost by making them less open with the press and less willing to provide those copious daily helpings of information. The press might become more argumentative and moralizing, but less generally informative, jettisoning all pretence to objectivity. Investigative reporting has already produced a strike force of self-proclaimed 'advocacy journalists', who use the press to espouse such causes as consumerism.

The search for crimes, conspiracies and cover-ups does not promise to be a very fruitful way of explicating the broader issues of public policy. Yet, because investigative reporting has become the glamorous assignment in the journalistic fraternity, the press gives the impression that all would be well were public officials not corrupt. It is a simple and morally satisfying view of the world, but it can be grossly misleading

The tendency of the press to focus on crime and corruption is not entirely new. Watergate exacerbated a tendency; it did not create one. American newspapers have always preferred a juicy scandal to the mundane details of budgets, taxation and legislation. Uncovering corruption has been the quick route to a Pulitzer Prize, the prestigious award for journalistic excellence. No doubt this preoccupation reflected the sad fact that government officials, especially those in local government, have not always shown a scrupulous regard for the distinction between the public purse and their private bank accounts. And since officials are not eager to prosecute themselves, it has been left to the press to bring public censure to bear. The archetypical case was the *New York World*'s exposé in the 1870s of the 'Tweed Ring', operated by Boss Tweed of the New York City Democratic Party. But while corruption is an enduring feature of municipalities, it gets more attention from the press than do subtler but at least equally important dysfunctions of urban government, including the ways in which it plans development, decides zoning patterns, builds highways, runs schools, and raises taxes.

Why do these issues not receive adequate attention from reporters? Part of the answer is the journalist's belief that readers would find such stories boring – certainly less interesting than a good scandal – and probably would not even understand them. The newspaperman's mental image of the average reader is a picture of a barely literate boor. Rowland Evans, a leading journalist, has described him thus: 'The average newspaper reader works in a Chicago steel mill, and his big occasion is Friday night at the local tavern with his wife and friends. Mostly he reads the comics and the sports.' Attempting to interest such a reader, newspapers emphasize those themes which might appeal to his supposedly limited comprehension: blood, sex and money.

Another part of the answer, although most journalists would be reluctant to admit it, is that newspapermen themselves have difficulty understanding the more complex processes that underly the day-to-day operations of government. American journalists have never been intellectuals until the last few decades higher education was not a prerequisite for the job. Aspiring reporters worked their way up from copy boy by displaying industriousness and perseverance not esoteric knowledge.

But the demands of the job are changing. The modern reader craves an understanding of the dynamics of inflation balance of payments and credit squeezes. He is curious about why there is a food shortage in the world and what can be done about it. If he is asked to conserve fuel, he wants to know the reason. To explain these complex phenomena, journalists need expertise in economics, agriculture, geology and other technical subjects. Some younger newspapermen are, in fact, arming themselves with graduate training. 'Speciality reporting' could challenge investigative reporting as the journalism of the future.

But it remains doubtful whether journalists, however good their intentions, can overcome the inherent contradiction between the complexity of the real world and the format of news presentation. Traditionally, a news story is supposed to simplify events for the reader, not merely serve them up with all their ambiguities showing. As Douglas Cater has observed, 'A reporter is a simplifier . . . he tends to ignore complexity when he can't understand it.' He does the same when he can understand it but despairs of being able to make the reader understand it. Yet the process of policy-making in government is full of subtleties: costs and benefits, alternatives and counter-alternatives. Since it is difficult for a journalist to deal with such shades of grey without feeling that he has confused readers even further he prefers whenever plausible to attribute the ills of society to corruption in high places, a clash of personalities, in-fighting among political cliques, and similarly dramatic causes.

Even the layout of the newspaper militates against sophisticated discussion of issues. Events must be graded by order of magnitude to determine the placement of stories on the page.

the size of the headline and the length of the text. But the standard of measurement is not the history of mankind, the last century or even the last decade: it is merely a single day. The consequent distortions become obvious if one imagines a day on which an important tax reform bill passes and an airliner crashes, killing 189 persons. The crash is interesting because it is sudden and dramatic and evokes sympathy for the victims. But its significance in the grand scheme of things is fleeting. It will be forgotten the next day. The tax bill, on the other hand, will have consequences for every citizen for a long time to come. But having dragged through Congress for many months, the tax bill is not really 'new' or dramatic. So the plane crash merits a big display and lengthy coverage as the important story of the day, while the tax bill becomes a relatively minor story.

The failings of the press are all the more disappointing when one considers what enviable freedom to enlighten and criticize it enjoys. The news media in America have been accorded a constitutional position of immunity that surely must be the envy of journalists labouring under more restrictive conditions elsewhere in the world. The First Amendment stipulates that 'Congress shall make no law abridging freedom of speech or of the press'. Because of it, nothing even remotely similar to the British Official Secrets Act or the system of D-notices hinders American newspapers. No suppression of news, no licensing of publishers nor taxation of newspapers (other than normal business taxes) may be imposed. Not even criminal trials are sheltered – although there have been attempts to do so – from the press's virtually absolute right to 'publish and be damned'.

The First Amendment was intended primarily to preclude prosecution of the common law crime of seditious libel. But, recognizing the crucial role of the press in the democratic order, the Supreme Court has read the amendment as a broad charter of editorial freedom. In a 1931 decision, *Near v. Minnesota* the justices declared in ringing terms that preventing publication by court order was the 'essence of censorship' and was prohibited by the First Amendment. Forty years later the court reaffirmed its stand against prior restraint of the press in the Pentagon Papers Case. A secret report recounting the political and military stratagems employed by the United States in Vietnam was stolen from the Defense Department by a former employee, Daniel Ellsberg, and given to the press. Although the official documents in question were purloined and although the attorney general asserted that their disclosure threatened 'national security', the court judged the government powerless to prevent their publication by the *New York Times* and the *Washington Post*. Justice Hugo Black, in one of the opinions in that case, observed that 'The Government's power to censor the press was abolished [by the First Amendment] so that the press would remain forever free to censure the Government. The press was protected so that it could bare the secrets of government and inform the people.'

Although protected against prior government censorship, the press might have been forced to censor itself if it could be held legally responsible for words already printed. But the Supreme Court has prevented public officials or even 'public figures' from recovering damages for a false and defamatory statement unless made 'with knowledge that it was false or with reckless disregard of whether it was false or not'. A similar test applies to reports published about private individuals incidentally connected with 'matters of public interest', such as victims of crimes. Few plaintiffs can meet that heavy burden of proof, which is precisely what the court intended, since it considered libel damages contrary to 'the principle that debate on public issues should be uninhibited, robust and wide-open'. The court has deemed it better to tolerate falsehoods than to deter free expression.

If there is a serious legal threat to freedom of the press today, it lies in the confrontation between journalists and the criminal courts. One source of conflict is the grand jury. Courts empanel grand juries to investigate suspected criminal activities and hand up indictments. The juries may subpoena witnesses, and those who refuse to testify after being granted immunity from prosecution can be convicted of contempt of court. Some grand juries have attempted to secure information about crimes by compelling journalists to testify, but the reporters have refused for fear of compromising their confidential sources and deterring others from talking to the press. Journalists contend that drying up confidential sources would defeat the public's 'right to know', a right which newsmen claim as a corollary of freedom of the press. Although at other times it has seemed convinced that the purpose of the First Amendment was a well-informed public, the Supreme Court in 1972 denied that there is a 'right to know' or that newsmen possess any special occupational privilege to refuse to testify before grand juries. Several states, however, have attempted to create that privilege by statute, enacting 'shield laws' to protect journalists from grand-jury questioning.

The reporting of criminal trials also brings journalists and the judiciary into conflict. There is no law that routinely restricts disclosure of the facts of a criminal case or the proceedings in the courtroom. It is generally agreed that such restrictions would violate the First Amendment. However, on a few occasions, judges who were concerned that newspaper accounts might prejudice the defendant's right to a fair trial have ordered journalists not to report certain crucial facts on pain of contempt. The constitutionality of these 'gag orders', like the shield laws, is not clear.

There is, however, a much more serious, if more subtle, threat to the free flow of news than judicial orders or grand jury investigations: the tendency of officials to 'classify' almost every document on the flimsy ground that its publication would not be in the public interest. All too often, as Justice Potter Stewart has observed, the classification system may be 'manipulated by those intent on self-protection or self-promotion'. To counteract the bureaucratic mania for stamping 'Classified', 'Secret', and 'Top Secret' on papers without any established criteria for doing so, Congress passed the

Freedom of Information Act in 1966. The act declared all federal documents open public records, except those dealing with personnel, private financial dealings, national security and criminal investigation. It requires officials to establish standards for deciding which documents are in the exempt categories and allows citizens to challenge these classifications in court. Congress, which often has trouble itself extracting information from bureaucrats, amended the act in 1974 to further broaden public access by disciplining officials who capriciously refuse to disclose information and allowing judges to examine all challenged documents *in camera* to determine if they are properly classified.

A favourable legal climate has been one important factor in the development of the American press. Another, perhaps equally important factor, is the structure of the newspaper industry. The striking feature of newspaper publication is that it is extremely localized. In Europe, the newspapers published in the capital or the larger cities are read throughout the country, but in America a person reads only the newspapers published in his own city. The circulation of the two most highly regarded newspapers in the country, the *New York Times* and the *Washington Post*, are confined almost exclusively to those two metropolises. A few persons outside New York do receive the *Times* by various means, but that accounts for only a small percentage of the readership. If the typical American reads a newspaper at all, it is almost invariably a local product, one of the approximately 1800 published daily across the country. Their circulation ranges from a few thousand to about one million; restricted to a single city, not even the mightiest American newspapers approach the multi-million readership of British and other European papers.

One consequence of localization is that most newspapers are not very good, since they lack resources. There is, however, a great diversity of editorial judgements, both in the 'play' that news events are given and in the opinion columns. At one time there was even more diversity; numerous newspapers competed vigorously in the large cities. But since the Second

World War, the economics of newspaper publishing has taken a heavy toll. Scores of newspapers merged with competitors or simply disappeared. New York City, which boasted nine dailies about twenty-five years ago, has now been reduced to three, and most cities have only one newspaper or one proprietor controlling all the papers in the same city. Competing dailies exist today in only about 10 per cent of the nation's 6000 cities and towns. Concentration of ownership has also taken the form of newspaper proprietors buying the local television stations. A number of 'chains', each controlling newspapers in several cities, have appeared. Even more damaging to diversity than concentrated ownership is the dependence of most newspapers on the two major wire services, the Associated Press and United Press International. Still, the very large number of newspapers assures that none can dominate the national reading public.

A second consequence of localization is the tendency to emphasize local news. Journalists follow the Newtonian principle that the gravity of events varies inversely with the distance from the readers. Sometimes the principle produces ludicrous results. An earthquake killing 200 persons in Africa is likely to get about as much attention from Chicago newspapers as a single pedestrian knocked down by a bus in Chicago. For that reason, news of foreign affairs tends to be woefully ignored by all but a few papers whose readers are presumed to rise above purely provincial concerns. Attention to local events, however, is consonant with the decentralized politics of a federal system. Readers are well served by a press which reports local politics as conscientiously – and usually more knowledgeably – as it does national politics.

The local emphasis, combined with the large number of newspapers, tends to dilute the impact of editorials. As de Tocqueville noted: '. . . [W]ith so many combatants, neither discipline nor unity is possible . . . Therefore American papers cannot raise those powerful currents of opinion which sweep away or sweep over the most powerful dykes.' Unlike European journals, American newspapers are not sharply divided along ideological lines nor do most of them maintain firm links with a political party. There is no 'party press' to speak of. The newspapers' neutral position has been achieved at least partly by having journalists who are largely liberal and Democratic work for proprietors who are mostly conservative and Republican. Newspapers do customarily endorse candidates in important elections, and since the editorials are generally the voice of the proprietors, newspapers tend to support Republicans. But the editorials strike readers with the force of a feather. That 75 per cent of all newspapers took a stand in favour of his opponent did not prevent John Kennedy from winning the Presidency. Newspaper support may carry somewhat more weight in minor elections, in which neither opponent is likely to be a celebrated figure, but generally what is said about a candidate in the news columns is far more persuasive than the imperial 'we' of the editorial pages.

If there is a 'national press', it consists of the *New York Times* (which despite its geographically limited readership is considered the newspaper of record), the three mass circulation newsmagazines – *Time*, *Newsweek* and *US News and World Report* – the three broadcasting networks, and two major wire services. That the magazines, wire services and networks, as well as the *Times*, have their headquarters in New York City within a few blocks of each other is partially responsible for the often expressed belief that an eastern liberal elite dominates the news media. However, the existence of hundreds of local newspapers makes it difficult for any elite, liberal or otherwise, to monopolize any given reader's intake of news.

Television is particularly open to the charge of elitism, because, although there are almost 700 independently owned television stations in the country, almost all are affiliated with one of the three commercial networks. While the local 'outlets' are responsible for local news programming, each broadcasts national news which is packaged in New York by the networks. In former days, when announcers merely read the headlines, network control of the news drew little attention. However, the networks have begun to do their own investigative reporting, and whenever a trenchant documentary appears, the subjects are likely to complain of unfairness.

Newspapers, which have no Press Council to contend with, may freely ignore such complaints, and they are quite inured to them. But television has no such immunity from sanctions. Newspapers were fortunate enough to have been invented by the late eighteenth century, when the First Amendment was written, but television was not. Therefore, Congress, with the acquiescence of the courts, has made 'electronic journalism' a thing apart from the branch of the trade which uses printing presses. The difference in technologies, perhaps, made governmental regulation of television inevitable. While myriad newspapers may compete for readers, television stations need to operate on exclusively assigned frequencies. Acting upon the theory that the airwaves were in the national domain, Congress, in the Federal Communications Act of 1934, parcelled them out to private enterprise (commercial broadcasting stations) much as it parcelled out the rights to exploit mineral deposits.

Naturally, a great many strings are attached to broadcasting licences. The Federal Communications Commission may deny or revoke a licence if it believes a broadcaster is not serving the public interest, convenience or necessity. For, as the Supreme Court said in 1969, 'it is the right of the viewers and listeners, not the right of broadcasters, which is paramount'. The FCC lays down guidelines for determining whether the broadcaster is, in fact, serving the public interest. The commission has, for example, required a certain minimum proportion of time to be devoted to news, and it has prescribed that the coverage be 'fair'. In some instances the commission requires persons mentioned unfavourably in news or commentary to be given free air time to reply. (No such burden may be placed on newspapers, the Supreme Court ruled in 1974, in striking down a state law that obliged them to print replies to editorial commentaries.) Thus, whenever complaints of 'unfairness' are lodged against television stations by viewers, the station has cause to fear for its very existence. In the past, licences have almost never been denied because of such complaints, but there are signs that 'viewer power' is gaining influence upon licensing decisions.

Government regulations is one reason why television is a less probing news medium than newspapers. Another is that newscasting is imbued with the values of the entertainment industry, of which the small screen is a part. Television newsmen prefer events that are simple and diverting to the eye. As a television executive has observed, 'If it didn't happen on film, it almost didn't happen.' Events like inflation, which are difficult to capture on film and more difficult to explain in thirty seconds, tend to be dismissed in brief bulletins. Moreover, television newsmen do not share the cynical, adversary tradition, that print journalists have had 200 years to develop. Television reporters are chosen for their beautiful faces and soothing voices rather than for their enterprising spirit, and few have had the rugged training that newspapermen undergo with demanding editors. As a result, television newsmen are not noted for asking penetrating questions.

That is all the more unfortunate since television has now replaced newspapers as the main news source for most persons. People tend to read newspapers for further details of stories that interest them, but their first, and often only, impression of events comes from the picture tube. Opinion research, moreover, indicates that Americans believe what they see on television more readily than what they read in the papers. Despite Walter Lippmann's conviction that the newspaper is the 'bible of democracy', it has never had quite the authority of holy writ; the accuracy of the news columns has always been doubted. The advent of television merely confirmed these doubts by persuading audiences that seeing is indeed believing.

Politicians have been quick to recognize the superior credibility of the electronic medium. Although they may ignore critical newspaper stories and hostile editorials, secure in the knowledge that few read or believe them, politicians are extremely anxious about their television image. President

Johnson kept three televisions in his office so that he could monitor all network news broadcasts simultaneously, and President Nixon often resorted to television, speaking to 'each and every one of you', in his effort to mobilize popular support. At the same time, he launched a vigorous campaign to discredit network newsmen for their allegedly prejudicial coverage of him. Among the practices which particularly irked Nixon was 'instant commentary' by newscasters following his television appeals. He felt, for good reason, that they negated the effect of what he had just said.

The Nixon critique did make television a bit more self-conscious about 'fairness' and perhaps caused it to bend over backwards to avoid slanting the news. Since, however, television already tends to err on the side of blandness rather than incisiveness, the net effect of excessive concern about fairness may be to strengthen the hand of those in the industry who would gladly abandon controversial news programming and documentaries altogether in favour of a steady, safe diet of quiz shows.

9 Elections: Throwing the Rascals Out

Americans enjoy elections. They may feign boredom when election time comes, but only because the campaign has not lived up to their expectations of a grand show. The best proof of how deeply elections are valued – or how much entertainment they afford – is the number of official posts which are filled by popular vote, rather than appointment. There are approximately 78,000 units of local government in the country, and even the most exiguous of these will have several elected officials. There are also state officials to be chosen, US representatives and senators to be selected and, capping it all, the Presidency to be filled. Even though a President is elected only once in four years, an election of some import to the voters occurs on the first Tuesday in every November.

The various levels of government are but one reason for the multitude of elective offices; another is that Americans are loath to fill any office without hearing the voice of the people. To an American, democracy means elections: balloting is a mechanism which, whatever its flaws, is the closest approximation to obtaining the consent of the governed. Thus, a great many officials are elected whom it might make more sense to appoint.

In most counties the sheriff, who is the chief law enforcement officer, is elected; so are the public prosecutor and the judges. Indeed, virtually the only participant in a criminal case who is not elected may be the defendant. Making a political issue of law enforcement has several undesirable consequences. Aspiring sheriffs make campaign promises to lock up more criminals, candidates for prosecutor pledge to prosecute unflinchingly, prospective judges vow on television to hand down severe sentences. Even if these candidates avoid making other private promises to their supporters, the normal currency of electoral politics, the maintenance of civil liberties and the impartiality of the judicial process are endangered by such campaigning.

Besides electing important officials who ought to be appointed, Americans spend a great deal of time and effort voting for persons to fill quite minor positions, especially at the state and local levels. Commissioners of water supply and commissioners of sewers are selected by the ballot box in many places; a community in the New York City suburbs duly elects commissioners to administer an escalator in a train station. Most members of school boards (education committees) are elected and their annual budget subjected to a referendum. State commissioners of parks and administrators of forests are sometimes elected officials. When one considers the variety of elective posts, the old American aphorism, 'he couldn't get elected dog catcher', does not really seem so far-fetched.

The combination of local self-government and elections for all offices does take its toll of the average citizen's powers of concentration. In the state of Oregon, for example, the voter is given a single paper ballot listing the candidates from President down to hamlet councillor; the paper is so huge that it is called a 'bedsheet ballot'. Under these conditions the theory of the informed voter choosing rationally among candidates whose position he knows is hardly accurate. The United States may have reached democratic overkill, the point at which so many elections are being held that no voter can possibly pay attention to them all.

The sheer volume of electoral politics helps explain the fragmentation of the two main parties. At the national level, the Republicans and the Democrats exist in name only. Each is a coalition of state and local organizations which carry the Republican or Democratic banners in their own bailiwicks. The parties may convene nationally every four years to nominate a presidential candidate, but in the years between, the local party organizations have their eyes fixed upon electing governors, mayors, county commissioners, state legislators and dozens of officials who mean more to their supporters in bread-and-butter terms than the President.

A monolithic, centrally controlled party with a well defined manifesto could hardly cope with so many electoral contests. Such a plethora of local issues need to be addressed that a rigid party line would limit a candidate's freedom of movement intolerably. In a British general election, every seat helps decide which party shall rule the country; even by-elections are taken as a sign of party strength nationally. But in America the local party organizations and candidates are engaged in campaigns whose national significance is usually minimal. They have little incentive for co-ordinating efforts with the party organization in the next county, let alone the next state.

Party politics is thus carried on primarily at the state and local level and only secondarily at the national level. The total number of representatives and senators elected for each party in these state contests does of course alter the balance of power in Congress, but the constituents vote mainly according to local political considerations. The closest equivalent to a British general election, the presidential election is the only contest where the issue is clearly national rather than local.

If the parties have no programme, then why bother with parties? For one thing, having no ideological commitment is not the same as having no goal. Parties have a very definite goal: seizing as many offices as possible. They also provide a vehicle for involving people in politics, even if only at the level of envelope-licker in campaign headquarters. For those who care about such things, participation yields a sense of having some influence on public affairs. For those who don't care, the parties perform the task of nominating candidates, removing the burden of having to decide for whom to vote. Because there is not much ideological content in American parties, the process of choosing one's party need not be a matter of rational choice at all. The very considerable effor which has been expended by American political scientists studying the voting behaviour of their compatriots indicates that party affiliation is generally inherited, along with social characteristics, like religion, race and income level, from one's parents and maintained because of one's friends and relatives. Thus, the social bases of the two parties differ, if not their theoretical underpinnings.

However, while there is a striking correlation between income level and party affiliation, Republicans and Democrats are not nearly as close to being class parties as are Labourites and Tories, primarily because ethnic as well as economic characteristics determine voting patterns. In general, the Republican party tends to be the party of the more affluent. The party draws its strength from small towns, suburbs of big cities and rural areas. Ethnically, the party is the stronghold of the WASP (White Anglo-Saxon Protestant), a term for Americans who trace their ancestry to early British, Germanic and Scandinavian settlers. The Democrats, on the other hand, are the party of the lower-income groups. Democratic strength is concentrated in the large cities, and the party has won the allegiance of the descendants of the post-Civil War immigrants who congregated there: Jews from Eastern Europe and Catholics from Ireland, Poland and Italy. The party has also enjoyed the disproportionate support of urban blacks. Until the late 1960s, the Democrats maintained a geographical bastion in the south. The region was dubbed the 'Solid South' by grateful Democrats, who reaped the benefits of the traditional resentment of the Republicans for their role in Reconstruction.

The Democratic coalition of ethnic groups was welded together by the Great Depression of the 1930s, but it has shown signs of strain because the components have developed some conflicting interests. The civil rights movement and the advent of black militancy have made blacks and southern whites reluctant partners, a tension which Nixon's 'Southern Strategy' of campaigning was intended to exploit. In the north, blacks and 'ethnics' have been at loggerheads over the issue of racial balance in the city school systems. A generation gap has also developed between the party's elders and its younger, college-educated generation, who are more insistent on promoting radical steps towards social equality; it was this generation which supported Eugene McCarthy's attempt to gain the democratic nomination in 1968 and who won the nomination for George McGovern in 1972. Both candidacies produced a split in the party, leaving it disunited in the presidential election.

The Democratic coalition has also been weakened by the increasing independence of the trade unions. In the 1972 presidential election the AFL–CIO conspicuously refrained from endorsing the Democratic candidate, and the Teamsters Union actually entered into a tacit alliance with President Nixon. The labour unions have come to believe that they have more to gain by staying independent and selling their support at a price to either side than by being permanent allies of the Democrats. Moreover, since many unions have been hostile to the attempt to foster black employment by 'minority recruiting programmes' which threaten union exclusiveness, the labourers' organizations have been susceptible to the siren call of the Southern Strategy.

Various third parties have cropped up throughout American history whenever large numbers of voters have deemed themselves unrepresented by either of the two main parties (Any party other than the Republicans and Democrats is termed a 'third' party; even a fourth party is generically a 'third' party.) They have proven ephemeral, however, because either the Republicans or Democrats usually move towards the position of the third party just enough to capture most of its supporters. When they do emerge, however, third parties can pose a serious threat to the major candidates. In 1968 Governor George C. Wallace amassed about 13 per cent of the votes cast, running as a candidate of the American Independent Party, enough to deny either main candidate a popular majority.

Typically, third parties are a response to 'Me-Too-ism'

the proclivity of the main parties to take nearly identical positions in their effort to stake out that vast middle ground where dwells the uncommitted voter. An indication of the size of the uncommitted middle may be gleaned from a 1975 Gallup Poll in which almost a third of voters classified themselves as 'independent'. No doubt many of these respondents pride themselves on their independence of mind while exhibiting a suspiciously consistent pattern of voting for the same party in every election. But it is fairly clear that the voter of no fixed affiliation, the voter who switches parties unpredictably from one election to the next, often decides presidential contests.

There is a large body of citizens whose political inclinations are unknown since they do not bother to trudge to the polling booths to register their views. In a presidential election more than 40 per cent of those eligible normally do not vote; in congressional elections the abstainees are even more numerous. According to the 'good citizen' theory of democracy, the apathy of so many signals danger, but some political sociologists have argued that those who do not vote are those with 'low commitment to democratic norms', that is people who might support a dictator if given the chance. Their failure to vote is a sign of contentment with democracy, the argument runs; their active participation in politics would be the real danger signal. Another theory is that those who fail to vote are caught between 'cross-pressures'. They may have one reason, such as ethnicity, for voting for one party, and another reason, such as economic status, for voting for the other party. They resolve their dilemma by staying home on election day. Despite these theories, however, what, if anything, is signified by the failure to vote remains a matter for sheer speculation. If it is difficult to explain the way people vote, it is even more difficult to explain the way they do not vote. About the only cause of non-voting that is patent is the weather; rain on election day is a notorious dampener of civic ardour.

The parties find their expression as national entities in that ultimate electoral spectacle, the presidential campaign.

Although winning the election gives the party control only of the executive branch, it is symbolically the equivalent of capturing the reins of government. As much energy and emotion are invested in that contest as in all other elections put together, and the number of people who participate either as delegates to nominating conventions or volunteer campaign workers runs into the hundreds of thousands.

The campaign begins just after the last election with sporadic declarations by the aspirants that they are *not* candidates for the Presidency. So many politicians have disavowed the office and then run for it that no one would be taken seriously unless he declared his non-candidacy early. Two years before the next election, the candidates formally enter the ring. The enormous length of time spent campaigning for the office has been criticized as a waste of effort which does nothing to enlighten the electorate but much to bore it, and politicians generally recognize the importance of having one's campaign 'peak' precisely on election day. Peaking too early means that the slogans have ceased seeming clever and the voter is tired of seeing the candidate's name on car bumpers. Strangely, all but the last two or three months of the campaign is spent in obtaining the nomination, so that often the final showdown between the party nominees seems somehow anticlimactic.

Winning the nomination essentially means persuading a majority of the 3008 delegates to the Democratic National Convention or the 2259 delegates to the Republican National Convention. Conventions are not mentioned in the constistution, which makes no provision at all for nominating presidential candidates, but they are among the strongest of the customary institutions. Until recently the delegates to the convention were chosen by the party organization in each state, usually meeting in a state convention. The national convention allowed a consensus on the presidential candidate to develop among state delegations unfamiliar with all the potential contenders. Delegates bargained in 'smoke-filled rooms', and numerous ballots were often required to select the candidate. But now that improved communications have made candidates' names household words, the convention appears to be searching for a new, more relevant function.

Since the old smoke-filled room is no longer a satisfying method of selection, there has been a growing tendency to make the choice more democratic by selecting the delegates themselves through primary elections or through state conventions which involve more than just party 'regulars'. By 1976, twenty-eight states had required Democrats and Republicans to select their delegates by primary election: a slate of proposed delegates committed to voting for Candidate X runs against slates committed to Candidates Y and Z. Most of these primaries are 'closed' in the sense that only registered members of a party can vote for delegates to its national convention. In a few states, the desire to maximize citizen participation has produced 'open' primaries in which a registered party member can 'cross over' to vote in another party's internal struggle. Until the law was changed in 1959, Californians could vote in *both* party primaries, a permissiveness which most politicians could not abide because it allowed the opposition to 'raid' a primary and saddle them with easily beatable candidates.

The states with primaries, however, supply only part of the convention delegates, so that the nomination ultimately may be decided by the representatives of the non-primary states. But the significance of the primaries goes far beyond the actual voting strength of the delegations so selected. (Some primaries are merely advisory, and some of those that bind the delegates to vote for the primary winner bind them only on the first convention ballot.) For the primaries give presidential aspirants, most of whom have successfully campaigned only within their own states as governors or senators, a chance to demonstrate their appeal as a national candidate.

In many instances, primary victories have been immensely persuasive. John F. Kennedy, then a senator from Massachusetts, was able, by winning the West Virginia primary in 1960, to dispel the fears of many Democratic politicians that a

Catholic would lose disastrously in predominantly Protestant states. At one stroke, he shattered the tenacious myth that a Catholic could never be elected President because of religious prejudice. In another momentous primary, Senator Eugene McCarthy persuaded President Johnson not to run for re-election by rolling up a sizable vote in New Hampshire in 1968.

It is not necessary, however, for a candidate to run in any primary. A candidate may choose to 'sit out' the primaries and do business on the convention floor, especially if he is a well-known figure who doesn't need the exposure or the ordeal by battle. For primaries pose a definite risk to a candidate. Victories are often inconclusive; they may be written off as idiosyncrasies or the product of peculiar circumstances. Senator Muskie's victory in New Hampshire in 1972 was not considered very convincing because he came from a neighbouring state. Defeat in a primary, however, always looks bad, and may prove conclusive. Hubert Humphrey's loss to Kennedy in the West Virginia primary crushed his chances of gaining the nomination in 1960.

Many valid objections have been raised against primaries. The states that have them, first of all, are not representative samples of the American electorate as a whole. Much attention is focused on the New Hampshire primary, held in February of the election year, because it is the nation's first. Yet no one would argue that a candidate acceptable to tiny New Hampshire, a rather eccentric state, is thereby the obvious choice of voters elsewhere. To make primaries more significant, it has been proposed that they be regionalized to include several states at once, obtaining a broader sample of the electorate. Rather than just New Hampshire, for example, all six New England states might hold primaries on the same day.

Another objection to primaries – especially before public funds began to be provided in 1976 – was that they emphasized the importance of a candidate's personal wealth. Deprived of any party funds, the primary candidate relied solely on his own bank account and on the contributions he could personally secure from political and family friends to buy television time and billboard advertisements, hire public relations firms, and pay for the travel of his retinue. The West Virginia primary is again a case in point: in proving his acceptability as a Catholic, Kennedy also demonstrated the importance of being a *rich* Catholic; while Kennedy travelled by air, Humphrey had to make do with a campaign bus.

There is also something disquieting about watching governors, senators, Vice Presidents and Presidents distract themselves from their official duties while they run in various states. As the *New York Times* lamented in an editorial in September 1975, 'With the national elections still fourteen months away, the country . . . faces the prospect of a President spending one third to one half – and eventually all – of his time crisscrossing the nation by jet plane in an endless round of speechmaking, handshaking, on-the-run news interviews and miscellaneous appearances.'

Winning primaries is only part of the candidate's task. He must also woo the delegates from the states which have no primaries. In these states the delegates are frequently chosen by a convention whose members have been selected by neighbourhood-level caucuses. In the past, powerful politicians, such as governors, senators and mayors, often controlled the state conventions and therefore the delegations chosen by them. Control by local strongmen is no longer as prevalent, but prominent politicians still influence the composition of delegations and provide much of their leadership. The diligent candidate, consequently, must tour the country, trying to convince the state leaders of his soundness on the issues and of his ability to win the election if chosen. As he listens to requests for his support, a delegation leader has one consideration uppermost in his mind: if he backs what turns out to be the winning candidate – and the earlier the better – his future access to the White House and the patronage and influence it holds, is assured, thereby strengthening his political position in his own state. But if he picks the loser, then he can expect no gratitude from the winning candidate. Early support of a candidate earns more influence, especially support which comes before it is apparent that he will carry the convention. Some leaders commit their troops early, others lead them into the convention hall as an 'uncommitted delegation', keeping all options open. It is common for a candidate to try to demoralize his opponents by claiming to have many delegates secretly committed to him, but these claims are usually exaggerated. His purpose is to create a 'bandwagon' effect, a panicky feeling among uncommitted delegates that the tide has turned in his favour and that they had better jump on the bandwagon or get left behind.

The campaign for the nomination comes to a climax at the convention, a boisterous, rowdy convocation of thousands of delegates, party officials, and onlookers, which is the only physical incarnation of the national party. Apart from choosing the presidential nominee, the convention serves a number of symbolic functions. The participants spend several days rousing themselves to a fine partisan fervour, with self-laudatory rhetoric, parades and (well-planned) 'spontaneous demonstrations' in favour of one candidate or another. The spirit thus generated is supposed to energize the party workers into making a strong effort on behalf of the nominee. For many participants the convention means a chance to have some fun as a reward for services rendered to the party; the crowd is swollen by alternate delegates, half-delegates and half-alternates, bespeaking an attempt to get as many as possible in on the revelry. (An alternate is provided in case a delegate is taken ill; half-delegates cast one-half vote and a half-alternate is his understudy.)

The convention also serves to air and sometimes resolve tensions that have developed within the party. There may be a battle in the credentials committee over which of two delegations from the same state represents the true party, requiring the national party to mediate between the state's warring factions. In 1964, for example, the Democratic credentials committee was faced with the choice of seating either all-white delegations from Alabama and Mississippi or all-black delegations sent by civil rights activists. With the wisdom of Solomon, the committee divided the seats between the competing delegations.

The convention's platform committee holds several days of hearings to demonstrate the party's openness to new ideas before formulating each of the 'planks', which when nailed together make a platform. The platform is invariably vague, so as to alienate as few voters as possible, and is quickly forgotten once it has been adopted by the full convention. Sometimes, however, the battle over the platform can focus hostile forces in the party, leading to serious disruption. In 1948 Southern Democrats or the 'Dixiecrats' withdrew from the convention because it adopted a mildly pro-civil rights plank and ran their own 'Dixiecrat' candidate.

But the main purpose of the convention is to pick the presidential nominee, which it does in one of three ways. If there is an obvious nominee, such as an incumbent President or a Vice President who is his heir apparent, the convention may simply choose him by acclamation. If there is a strong but not certain candidate, it may take only one ballot to obtain a majority. Single-ballot conventions have become usual in recent years because of the intensive cultivation of delegates beforehand. But in the past it has required numerous ballots for a candidate to be nominated. In 1924, when party rules required a two-thirds majority, the Democrats took 102 ballots. If a candidate fails to secure a majority on the first ballot, it may shatter the bandwagon effect he has carefully nurtured and cause a 'stampede' of delegates to another candidate. When two or more strong candidates fail to overcome each other after numerous ballots, the party may turn to a 'dark horse', a relatively obscure politician whom all sides can agree upon as a compromise candidate.

When the presidential candidate has been chosen, the convention has one more important piece of business before adjourning: choosing his 'running-mate', the nominee for Vice President. Because the Vice President is normally an inconsequential figure (with no important duties), the convention has usually opted for the person who would strengthen the 'ticket', attracting votes to the presidential candidate by virtue of his personal political following. Whether the vice presidential nominee would also make a good President is a decidedly secondary consideration, which explains why there is always some queasiness when a Vice President succeeds a President; everyone is quite aware of how one gets to be Vice President.

Usually the convention attempts to balance the ticket by selecting a vice presidential candidate who is everything that the presidential nominee is not – ideologically, ethnically and geographically. If the presidential candidate is a liberal, then it is considered prudent to select a conservative for Vice President. If he is from the east, then a westerner might be chosen to run for Vice President. If one is a Protestant, the other ought to be a Catholic. Such arrangements assure that there will be something for everyone on the ticket, although perhaps at the cost of knowing what the ticket really stands for. An obvious method of consolidating support for the ticket is to have the presidential nominee choose his leading rival for the nomination as his running mate. Serving as 'standby equipment', as a potential vice presidential candidate once disdainfully put it, may not appeal to the rival, who would rather maintain his current electoral power base. Lyndon Johnson was reluctant to accept the Democratic vice presidential nomination when offered it by John F. Kennedy in 1960, because, at first blush, Johnson considered himself better off remaining as the Senate majority leader.

Since so many Vice Presidents have become Presidents in recent decades, concern has mounted about the customary manner of selecting Vice Presidents, in which all long-range considerations of his suitability to become chief executive are sacrificed to immediate political requirements. Most of the time, in fact, the convention does not really evaluate the candidate; it simply ratifies automatically whoever the presidential nominee desires for a running mate. In future conventions, however, the question may be thrown open to a floor debate, because, for one thing, the Twenty-fifth Amendment has demonstrated how much more satisfying it can be to know something about the second-highest official before he is thrust into office. Under the amendment, whenever the Vice Presidency becomes vacant, the President can nominate a successor, who must be confirmed by both houses of Congress. That provides an opportunity for minute scrutiny of the candidate. When Gerald Ford was designated, his personal life, career, finances, and congressional voting records were examined intensely in the Senate and House of Representatives. Having obtained their bi-partisan imprimatur, Ford was a known quantity, so that when he replaced President Nixon there was little of the uneasiness that had attended the succession of some popularly elected Vice Presidents. Unlike them, Ford had not been chosen as an afterthought late one night during a frenzied political convention.

Haphazard selection of Vice Presidents is only one of the flaws in the system of nomination by convention, a traditional mechanism which many now feel to be inherently undemocratic and outdated. The main purpose of the convention had always been to provide an indirect method of selecting among candidates who, in the pre-electronic age, were but vague names to most voters. Today, however, a convention is no longer needed to make the faces of presidential contenders familiar. They are on television for many months before the convention. A democratic alternative would be to select the candidates directly in a single nation-wide primary, but more problems might be created than were solved. If all of the contenders were listed on the ballot, none would be likely to obtain a majority, leading to cumbersome runoff elections and bargaining among the candidates for each others' support – which is essentially what happens at a convention.

Although the convention, for lack of anything better, is thus likely to survive for some time to come, there are indications that it may evolve into an institution more compatible with modern notions of democratic participation. In 1974, the Democrats adopted a party charter which encourages participation by minority group members, women and young voters in the delegate selection process; more of these persons, presumably, will serve as delegates themselves. Conventions should cease to be dominated by white, middle-aged males. The charter also introduced a system of proportional representation, under which each state delegation will contain members supporting a variety of candidates, in proportion to their strength in the primaries or state nominating conventions. The result should be a more open convention. No longer will a few state leaders, commanding regiments of committed delegates, be able to broker the nomination. There will still be bargaining, but the bargainers will be more numerous and their individual power more attenuated.

By gaining the nomination at the convention, the presidential candidate acquires control of the national party apparatus: its staff, academic advisers, funds, and field workers. But most important of all, he acquires the party name. Since party identification appears to be a potent influence on voting, the label will account for most of his support. Whether a candidate chooses to emphasize his party affiliation above other attributes is a matter of strategy. In general, since the Democratic Party has more registered members than does the Republican, the Democratic candidate is much more likely to beat the drums of party loyalty, even at the risk of losing some Republican supporters. But the candidate's personality and reputation are also important. Unlike those who run for lesser offices, presidential candidates are celebrities by the time they emerge from the convention.

The final campaign, which lasts from the beginning of September until early in November, strives to rally the party faithful to the cause and to convert that portion of the electorate, which has little or no party identification. Many of these voters make their decision in the two months preceding election day, according to the pollsters, who keep a finger pressed to the public pulse as the campaign progresses. To persuade the uncommitted to decide the right way, it is necess-

ary for the candidate either to turn on his personal charm or to
tar the opposition with responsibility for the nation's ills.
The latter is an effective line of attack, because voters seem to
turn out in unusually large numbers when they wish to vote
against something; they often neglect to vote for candidates
towards whom they feel well-disposed. It is helpful to a
candidate for the polls to report that he has a good chance of
winning, since Americans do not like voting for certain losers.
Here is the bandwagon effect writ large: the voters find it so
distasteful to be associated with the losing side that they
switch to the predicted winner, thus fulfilling the prediction.

Candidates assiduously avoid taking strong stands on issues
(the party platform has by now been consigned to oblivion)
or making specific proposals, since that might alienate uncommitted voters. The presidential campaign of Senator
Barry Goldwater in 1964 demonstrates the consequences of
ignoring this precept. Rather than concern itself with maximizing votes, the Goldwater campaign organization professed
an uncompromising right-wing ideology. To secure purity of
doctrine, it purged the Republican party ranks of dissidents.
The candidate took strong positions on issues such as race
relations and the Vietnam War. Goldwater even went so far
as to tell special audiences precisely what they did not want to
hear. He opposed Social Security pensions in Florida, where
a great many of the nation's pensioners live, and he attacked
the Tennessee Valley Authority as 'creeping socialism' in a
speech in Tennessee, which owes much of its prosperity to
the authority's hydro-electric generators. All this was to
present the electorate, in Goldwater's words, with 'a choice,
not an echo'. The voters chose. His opponent, Lyndon
Johnson, won a landslide victory, and the Republican Party
was so severely wounded that one commentator hailed the
emergence of the 'one-and-a-half-party system'.

More typically, candidates assess the problem before them
as one of discovering how best to appeal to an electorate
which is divided into discrete interest groups. They think of
voters in ethnic categories (the Jewish Vote, the Irish Vote),

occupational groupings (the Farmers, the Businessmen), geographical compartments (the Eastern Vote, the Midwestern Vote), and demographical categories (the Urban Vote, the Rural Vote). They try to tailor their campaign by mailings, by phone and personal canvassing and by television and newspaper advertisements, so as to appeal to each category separately, gambling that the others are not listening. The same candidate may advertise in rural newspapers, urging higher farm prices, and then appear on television in the cities to decry high food costs.

The use of television by presidential contenders is steadily increasing, despite the absence of any real proof, other than the politician's hunch, that it does a candidate much good. There is some agreement that it can do him a great deal of harm because television emphasizes the visual appeal of candidates rather than what they are saying. 'Television,' Vice President Rockefeller once observed, 'is a very revealing medium,' and often what it reveals is not very attractive. In the televised 'Great Debates' of the 1960 election between Nixon and Kennedy, Nixon made a relatively poor impression because he looked tense and because his face, despite the best efforts of razor and powder puff, had an ominously shadowy appearance. Kennedy's boyish countenance and floppy hair, in contrast, gave him a more pleasing television personality.

Judging from the fact that no 'Great Debates' have been held in any campaign since, candidates have apparently concluded that debating is strewn with pitfalls. Nixon, who was a candidate in two more elections, did not repeat his error. Instead of debating, he purchased air time for question-and-answer sessions before audiences packed with his supporters. In this controlled setting, knowing the questions in advance and surrounded by sympathetic faces, he felt that he projected his best image, that of an experienced statesman.

At election time, such 'packaging' of political candidates at all levels becomes a boom industry, captained by a new breed of professional political advisers known as 'media men'. Bringing to bear all the skills acquired through decades of selling deodorant soaps and dog food, these electoral *condottiere* show the candidate how to condense his virtues into a sixty-second spot commercial. The overt message is as innocuous as a jingle; the real object is subliminal persuasion. Looking relaxed and affable, often with his jacket off and tie loosened, the candidate is portrayed in amiable conversation with voters. The viewer is supposed to receive the impression that here is a man of the people, at home with common folk and sensitive to their problems. A common technique (especially if the opponent is single) is to display the candidate at home, surrounded by his wife, children and pets, so as to convey an aura of respectability and stability.

Waging political warfare by means of commercials does have the advantage of translating the electoral process into the familiar idiom of a popular culture medium. Fears that slick showmanship may mesmerize the electorate are quite unfounded, since even children, reared on television commercials, understand their ulterior motives and tendency to deceive by half-truths and exaggerated claims.

But commercials hardly raise the level of political discourse. The merchandising of presidential candidates may also discourage more reflective persons from seeking the office. After campaigning for the 1976 Democratic nomination for almost a year, Senator Walter F. Mondale, a Minnesota liberal, announced he was withdrawing from the race because he could not force himself to conduct the kind of campaign that was required. Mondale explained:

> Nationally, it's more theatre than the politics I know. I kept getting constant suggestions that I needed to buy different clothes and go to speech instructors and spend two days in Hollywood with a videotape machine. I hated that.

But the most daunting aspect of presidential campaigning is the raising of funds. 'Money,' a veteran politician once remarked, 'is the mother's milk of politics,' but during the

1960s and the 1970s the candidates' need for this nourishment grew inordinately. In the 1972 election, the Republican candidate spent $61 million and the Democratic $39 million. Requiring such huge sums made candidates dependent on 'fat cats', large contributors who are thus in a position to demand political favours. The possibilities for corruption have not been underexploited. Investigations of the 1972 campaign revealed dozens of clandestine, illegal contributions by corporations; a suitcase stuffed with hundred-dollar bills seemed to be the standard unit of contribution.

Provoked by such blatant examples of cloak-and-dagger campaign financing, Congress enacted in 1974 a reform bill which promised to change radically the relationship between private money and presidential politics. Each major-party candidate is limited to spending $20 million, the full amount of which is provided by the US Treasury, making private contributions unnecessary. In presidential primaries, candidates are limited to spending $10 million. The Treasury provides up to half that amount, matching whatever contributions the candidate gains from private sources. The role of the 'fat cats' is drastically reduced because no individual may give any candidate more than $1000. (The law also set spending limits for congressional campaigns but provided no public funds.)

The law was substantially modified in 1976 by a ruling of the Supreme Court, which held that campaign spending was a form of political expression protected against government restriction by the freedom-of-speech provision of the First Amendment. Significantly, the court did not find that the limit on contributions to candidates was an unconstitutional restriction on the *donor's* freedom of speech. The ruling abolished expenditure limits for congressional elections, but the practical import for presidential elections may not be great since the court stipulated that any candidate who voluntarily accepts the campaign subsidies may be held to the spending limit. In the 1976 election, all candidates accepted the money proferred by the Treasury.

The strategy of campaigning is heavily influenced by the fact that technically the President is not elected by direct popular vote, but indirectly through the electoral college. Under Article II of the Constitution, a group of electors, one for each senator and representative in the state's congressional delegation, are chosen in each state to cast ballots for President. When the constitution was first put into practice the electors were actually free agents; they could cast their votes for whoever they chose. Today there are slates of would-be electors, committed to a particular candidate. When that candidate wins the majority of the popular vote in any state, the whole slate of electors committed to him is thereby selected.

Although the electoral-college system gives disproportionate weight to small-population states – New York has sixty times the population of Alaska, but only fifteen times as many electoral votes – the net effect of the winner-take-all rule is to make the populous states crucial to a candidate. If he can win the popular majority in New York by even a single vote, he acquires all forty-three of its electoral votes. If he can win the dozen most populous states, even narrowly, he can secure a majority of the 535 electoral votes in the nation. Candidates naturally tend to concentrate their efforts on these pivotal states. A mathematically imaginative team of political scientists has calculated that voters in California, the most populous state, are '2.92 times as attractive campaign targets' as voters in the least populous state. In fact, politicians native to the populous states are often preferred as nominees because they start with such a great advantage.

The electoral-college system produces some curious distortions in the voting process. Although it is an antique and anti-democratic institution, the system affords liberals and minority groups exceptionally potent leverage in a presidential election, because they live in urban areas that dominate the states with large blocs of electoral votes. Winning the cities and their suburbs, means carrying off all the electoral votes of the big states. The prudent candidate thus concentrates on cultivating the urban vote and pays attention to the interests of urbanites.

The electoral system leaves open the possibility that a candidate who gains the majority of popular votes nationally will nevertheless lose the election because he fails to amass a majority of the electoral votes. It has happened only once before, in the election of 1876, when Samuel J. Tilden, who held a 250,000-vote margin in the popular balloting, lost by one electoral-college vote. Such a discrepancy between popular and electoral votes may occur when a candidate wins the populous states by slim margins and loses the sparsely inhabited states by large margins. The narrow victories earn him far more electoral votes than his overall performance warrants. (The disparity between electoral and popular vote totals can be enormous. In 1968, Hubert Humphrey polled 42.7 per cent of the popular vote and 191 electoral votes while his opponent, Richard Nixon, polled 43.4 per cent of the popular vote and 301 electoral votes.)

A similarly undemocratic outcome might result if no candidate gained an absolute majority of the electoral votes, which is likely when more than two persons run. In the absence of a majority, the constitution provides that the President shall be chosen by the House of Representatives from among the three candidates with the highest electoral totals. But here the principal of sovereign equality of the states reasserts itself, for each state delegation in the House casts a single vote. Alaska, in other words, casts one vote, and so does New York, which has sixty times Alaska's population. A President could therefore be chosen, theoretically, by the delegations of the twenty-six smallest states, representing about 15 per cent of the nation's population.

Another worrisome, albeit remote, possibility is that the electors might undo the result of the popular voting by casting their ballots for a candidate other than the one to whom they were nominally committed. Pledging of votes has become customary, but it is not a legally binding obligation. In the presidential elections of 1948, 1964 and 1968, one elector changed his mind. So far these aberrations have not influenced the outcome of a contest.

Several constitutional amendments to eliminate the undesirable consequences of the electoral system have been proposed. One would abandon the electoral college entirely and elect the President by direct, popular vote. The major obstacle would be the need for a single, national election register. The states, which are constitutionally responsible for determining the qualifications for voting, would be unlikely to acquiesce in such an infringement of their prerogatives. However, by granting the vote to eighteen-year-olds in every state, the Twenty-sixth Amendment, adopted in 1971, set a precedent for overriding state discretion and creating a homogeneous presidential electorate.

Another proposal would modify the electoral college by allocating one electoral vote to each congressional district and permitting the winner-take-all system to operate only within a district. The disparity between popular and electoral vote totals would be reduced, since congressional districts are roughly equal in population, but the presidential outcome might then be merely a reflection of the congressional race. Since the Democrats have fairly consistently held a majority of seats in Congress, the Republicans might well fear the consequences of electing Presidents in a similar manner. (On the other hand, congressional elections might become a reflection of presidential elections, which would be welcome to the Republicans.)

A third proposal is to establish proportional representation, assigning each candidate electoral votes in proportion to his share of popular votes in each state. It would abolish altogether disparities between the popular and electoral votes. But it would also have the effect of shifting influence away from the populous urban states and towards the more sparsely inhabited states, because the large electoral blocs of the former would be split among Republicans and Democrats. Since the Democrats now tend to be more successful in capturing these blocs, they would be unlikely to look with favour upon proportional representation. Given the lack of consensus for any of these reforms of the electoral college, the system is likely to continue unchanged until the dire prophecies of a serious malfunction come true.

10 Man Versus the State

All nations constantly confront the problem of drawing the line between the rights of individuals and the interests of the state. The way in which they do so is often the distinctive mark of their system of government. As Federal Judge Jerome Frank has said, 'The test of the moral quality of a civilization is its treatment of the weak and the powerless.' More than most countries, the United States is imbued with a reverence for civil liberties. The Declaration of Independence spoke of man's 'inalienable rights', and the framers of the constitution designed checks and balances to prevent the federal government from becoming a tyranny. So content were the framers with the basic structure that they saw no need for specific guarantees.

Denouncing the 'injudicious zeal for bills of rights', Alexander Hamilton argued in the *Federalist Papers* that the 'constitution is itself . . . a bill of rights'. Recalling that Magna Carta and the Petition of Right were stipulations by monarchs, Hamilton maintained that a bill of rights would ill suit a democratic constitution, in which 'the people surrender nothing'. He contended that a bill of rights was less necessary to a constitution 'merely intended to regulate the general political interests of the nation, than to a constitution which has the regulation of every species of personal and private concerns'. Finally, Hamilton warned, a bill of rights is more than unnecessary; it is dangerous. The provisions would be construed as exceptions to powers that must by implication exist: 'For why declare that things shall not be done which there is no power to do?' With the wisdom of hindsight, it is obvious that Hamilton underestimated the scope of the powers which the government eventually would exercise and the consequent menace to individual liberty. The provisions of the American bill of rights have indeed been construed as mere exceptions to powers. But the authority of government has grown inexorably since Hamilton's time, and were it not for the bill of rights there would be no exceptions.

To give him his due, Hamilton was certainly justified in claiming that even without a bill of rights the constitution was not devoid of specific prohibitions against infringement of liberty. Article I, in setting forth the legislative power, forbids suspending the writ of *habeas corpus* or passing bills of attainder and *ex post facto* laws. Article III, the judicial article, provides for the trial of all crimes by jury and lays down strict rules of proof for treason trials. Article IV guarantees 'the citizens of each state shall be entitled to all privileges and immunities of citizens in the several states', and Article VI prohibits imposing a religious test for holding public office. Taken as a whole, however, this catalogue of assorted proscriptions hardly amounts to a comprehensive charter of liberties, and one might legitimately ask: if these specific limits need be spelled out in writing, why not all the others?

Hamilton's arguments were in vain. To win support for the proposed constitution, its supporters were obliged to accede to the public demand for a bill of rights. Adopted in 1791, two years after ratification, the bill took the form of a package of ten amendments, most of which are negative in tone. They do not say 'the citizen shall have the right to . . .' Rather, they are couched in terms of prohibitions against specific kinds of government acts. The bill of rights is thus much less sweeping and idealistic than some charters of liberty, such as the United Nations Universal Declaration of Human Rights, which lays down broad positive rights, but it is therefore much more difficult to circumvent. With the bill of rights, the early Americans hedged their bet on democracy and majority rule. They declared some measures out of bounds, even if a majority desired them, in order to guarantee that the minority would at least survive the consequences of not being on the winning side. If democracy is defined as pure majoritarianism, then the bill of rights is undemocratic; but if democracy is held to subsume the concept of legitimate opposition, then the bill is a fundamental part of the democratic scheme. America is, as Professor Henry J. Abraham has put it, a 'constitutional democracy, based upon a government of limited powers under a written constitution, and a majoritarianism duly checked by carefully guarded minority rights.'

In laying down these protections for dissenting minorities, the bill of rights speaks with firmness. A provision which begins 'Congress shall make no law' leaves little doubt that the safeguard is to be unqualified. But specific as well as broadly worded provisions require interpretation in concrete cases, and that is the job of the courts. Whenever anyone believes that the federal or state governments has violated the bill of rights, causing him personal harm, he may take his complaint to the judiciary. As the apex of the judicial pyramid, the Supreme Court has become the primary guardian of the rights of Americans.

While the meaning of the bill of rights may be altered by judicial interpretation, no provision is made for its abrogation in times of war or 'national emergency' in order to permit summary trials, internment or censorship. The guarantees can only be removed by formally amending them. That the republic has stood so long without ever rescinding its bill of rights, even temporarily, may perhaps be taken as a rebuke to all those who believe that civil liberties must be the first casualty of national distress.

On the other hand, the executive and legislative authorities sometimes take whatever steps they deem necessary in time of emergency, secure in the expectation that the court will find no conflict with the bill of rights when it later reviews those steps. Japanese-Americans, including native-born citizens, were summarily rounded up on the Pacific Coast and shipped to internment camps during the Second World War upon the orders of President Roosevelt. Although that was a clear infringement of the right to due process of law, when the Japanese Exclusion Order was challenged at the end of the war, the Supreme Court upheld it. Dissenting, Mr Justice

Murphy expressed what was probably the real sentiment of the bench when he said that the action 'falls into the ugly abyss of racism'. But in his opinion for the majority, Mr Justice Black, normally an avid libertarian, alluded to the difficulty of judicial review of emergency actions: 'We cannot – by availing ourselves of the calm perspective of hindsight – now say that at that time these actions were unjustified.'

But on the whole, civil liberties have been staunchly protected by the courts because of an underlying belief that they are vital to the health of the political order – not idealistic encumbrances on effective government. No better illustration can be found of the nexus between civil liberties and American democracy than the First Amendment, which provides:

> Congress shall make no law respecting an establishment of religion, or prohibiting the free exercise thereof; or abridging the freedom of speech, or of the press; or the right of the people peaceably to assemble, and to petition the Government for a redress of grievances.

The freedoms of religion, speech, press, assembly and petition are called the 'preferred freedoms', because they allow that vigorous exchange of ideas upon which, according to classic libertarian theory, democratic government thrives. In balancing the rights of citizens against the needs of the state, the court gives greater weight to the 'preferred freedoms' than to some other civil liberties because ultimately the survival of the democratic form of government depends on their maintenance.

Freedom of religion is included among these because religion, like political belief, is properly a matter of conscience and because religious intolerance has been a traditional cause of persecution. The 'establishment clause' of the First Amendment precludes an identification between church and civil authorities, although it has been argued that the intent was merely to prevent the *federal* government from creating an official church that would compete with those that the states might wish to establish. From the earliest days, America had been a haven for refugees from religious persecution, and although some colonies were known to expel a heretic from time to time, the nation as a whole had to face the fact that it was composed of a multitude of faiths.

An atheist might cast a jaundiced eye upon the history of the establishment clause, since it has not prevented government from promoting and sustaining organized religion. Churches and their property have always been exempted from taxation, undoubtedly a beneficial concession. Reaffirming the validity of this traditional practice, the Supreme Court held in 1970 that by granting tax exemption the government 'simply abstains from demanding that the church support the state'.

The relationship between religion and education poses a more prickly question. The court has discerned no breach in the wall of separation between church and state when the latter provides free transportation and textbooks for pupils in church-run schools as well as state schools. But it has found a violation of the establishment clause when the state provides funds for the salaries of church-school teachers, even teachers of secular subjects. Although it may be difficult to understand that distinction, the principle is that the state must maintain 'neutrality' in matters of religion. It may supply books and bus rides to all pupils; where they use them – church or state schools – is their own choice. But paying teachers is a direct state subsidy to a religious institution.

The companion to the establishment clause, the free exercise clause, is a less contentious provision except in the case of small sects which claim not only the freedom to believe but the freedom to act according to their beliefs. The Jehovah's Witnesses alone have been at the centre of about forty Supreme Court cases. In most of those the court has upheld their right to behave unconventionally in order to fulfil the tenets of their faith. They are permitted to proselytize aggressively, even when it causes a nuisance to others, and their children are permitted to refuse to salute the flag in school, thus avoiding the sin of idolatry. But again the lines are blurred. Jews may not violate Sunday closing laws even though they close their businesses on a different sabbath, but Seventh Day Adventists are entitled to unemployment benefits when their unemployment results from conscientious refusal to work on Saturdays.

Even more than freedom of religion, freedom of speech is regarded as vital to the healthy functioning of democracy, because it provides the 'marketplace of ideas' in which the nation shops for public policy. And it assures, as the Continental Congress said in 1774, that 'oppressive officers are shamed or intimidated into more honourable and just modes of conducting affairs'. For these reasons the court has given freedom of speech the greatest possible scope when it involves issues of public concern. Newspapers are constitutionally exempt from prior censorship, and the court has made it virtually impossible for a government official to sue successfully for libel or slander, lest such penalties have a 'chilling effect' on the discussion of public issues.

Despite the absolute language of the First Amendment, however, the court has carved out several exceptions to freedom of speech and the press in instances where speech seems to go beyond contributing to the theoretical marketplace. One exception is speech that presents a 'clear and present danger' of producing harmful consequences which the government has a duty to prevent. Using 'fighting words' to harangue a crowd into violent action or reaction and inciting others to violently overthrow the government is not constitutionally protected speech. The court thus allowed the prosecution of the Communist Party as subversive, although the justices ultimately drew a distinction between direct incitement to revolutionary acts and mere 'abstract advocacy and teaching of forcible overthrow'. The court was also notably unwilling to prevent the House Un-American Activities Committee from conducting an inquisition for almost forty years into the political beliefs of those it suspected of communist sympathies. By the time it was abolished in 1975, the committee had subpoenaed and publicly interrogated thousands of 'hostile witnesses', an episode whose chilling effect upon free speech amounted to an Ice Age.

The court has also drawn a careful distinction between pure speech, which is protected, and speech mixed with physical action, which is not. While the citizen is entitled to certain forms of 'symbolic speech' that partake of action, such as carrying a picket sign, he may not claim shelter under the First Amendment for engaging in a disruptive sit-in. The line between symbolic speech and action is exceedingly fine. Burning an American flag as a gesture of protest is permissible, but burning a military draft card is not.

Another exception to freedom of speech is the publication of obscenity. The doctrine that obscenity is not speech protected by the First Amendment has been extremely controversial since it was enunciated in 1957 because it legitimized censorship during a period when social and cultural mores were undergoing a drastic transformation. But the court reasoned, in the words of Justice Brennan, that 'implicit in the history of the First Amendment is the rejection of obscenity as utterly without redeeming social importance', and the justice noted a 'universal judgement that obscenity should be restrained'. No better illustration can be found of the utilitarian concept of the First Amendment than the notion that freedom of expression exists only to fulfil the specific function of enhancing democratic government. That speech might also provide a medium for cultural and artistic expression seems to have been ignored by the court. Nevertheless, the justices found it much easier to outlaw obscenity than to define it, and many books, magazines and films have escaped censorship via the loophole of 'redeeming social importance'. By the early 1970s the court had decided to allow each locality to judge for itself what the prevailing moral sentiments of the community were, a step which relieved the bench of the role of film and book reviewer but which raised the chaotic possibility that a best-selling novel in one city would be banned as pornographic in another.

By a stroke of sheer bathos, the First Amendment, with its broad guarantee of free debate, is followed immediately by an amendment which assures the citizen's right to bear arms.

The intent was to allow part-time militias to be maintained, and perhaps to remind the governors what might happen if they lost the consent of the governed. In any event, the Second Amendment helped ensure that today's governors would face a heavily armed population – millions of handguns and rifles are in circulation – whose weaponry would be more commonly used in the commission of crimes than in the defence of civil liberties. By enshrining Americans' natural attraction to firearms as a fundamental freedom, the bill of rights has made it more difficult to enact laws which would restrict the free circulation of guns, thereby reducing the incidence of fatal violence.

The Third Amendment, which prohibits quartering troops in private homes, testifies to the bad memories left by the compulsory lodging of British troops in the homes of the colonists. But in an era when the Defense Department lavishes billions of dollars upon domestic and foreign bases, the possibility of lodging its divisions in spare bedrooms here and there seems quite remote. The Third Amendment is thus little more than an historical curiosity.

The Fourth Amendment, prohibiting unreasonable searches and seizures, was also a reaction to a British colonial practice, that of issuing general warrants empowering officers to search anywhere on the slightest pretexts. But, unlike the Third Amendment, it has assumed a great importance in modern America. The core of the amendment is the warrant procedure: the police must go before a judge to show that they have probable cause to believe that a crime has been committed, justifying a search. They must also specify where the search is to take place, the names of the suspects, and the evidence they are seeking. The amendment is thus one of the main safeguards against arbitrary police practices, especially since the court early in the 1960s began to apply the 'exclusionary rule' in state as well as federal trials. A judicial invention, the exclusionary rule makes any evidence uncovered by the police in a manner prohibited by the Fourth Amendment inadmissible in a subsequent trial. Denied the fruits of unconstitutional searches, the police are effectively deterred from carrying them out.

Although written at a time when physical entry was the only method of search, the Fourth Amendment has been 'adapted' to meet analogous threats to privacy posed by modern technology. Freed of the shackles of literal interpretation, the Fourth Amendment now protects against wiretapping, eavesdropping and other electronic means of surveillance as well as physical intrusions, and it guards individuals in public places as well as on private premises. An invisible bubble of privacy encases the citizen wherever he may be. The amendment, in fact, supplies the foundation upon which the court has constructed a right to privacy that goes far beyond police investigations and encompasses such civil liberties as the right to an abortion. Unfortunately, since the exclusionary rule remains the chief instrument for enforcing the amendment, the unhappy implication is that only suspected criminals have a routinely enforceable right to privacy.

That other than criminal suspects need such protection has become quite clear. The Rockefeller Commission reported in 1975 that the Central Intelligence Agency had for about twenty years engaged in illegal spying upon thousands of Americans. The CIA had tapped phones, planted 'bugs', burglarized homes and intercepted letters without warrants. Since the information was gathered for the purpose of 'counterespionage' – i.e., disruption of dissident political groups – rather than prosecution, the CIA was undeterred by the exclusionary rule. Perhaps the only way to protect the rights of citizens against such illegal surveillance would be, as the Rockefeller Commission recommended, to assure closer presidential and congressional oversight of intelligence operations.

Amendments V, VI, VII and VIII provide for 'due process of law' in judicial proceedings, especially criminal trials. A reaction to the memory of the royal Star Chamber, whose primary method of establishing guilt was to torture the accused into confessing, the amendments assure a defendant the right to indictment by grand jury and to speedy, public trial by jury. He also has the right to be represented by counsel, to confront and cross-examine witnesses against him, and to compel by subpoena the appearance of favourable witnesses. The defendant may not be forced to testify against himself and may not be tried again for the same offence once acquitted. He is protected against 'excessive' bail and fines and 'cruel and unusual punishments'.

Most of these rights were enormously expanded by the court, in practical terms during recent decades because of a growing realization that the judicial system operated unfairly against the poor and uneducated. The right to remain silent and to representation by counsel might protect those who knew they could refuse to give the police statements when arrested and who had the means to hire a lawyer. But these rights meant little in practice to the ignorant, impoverished person who neither knew he could keep silent nor had the money to secure representation. Since the police often took advantage of a suspect's ignorance in their zeal to obtain convictions, the court decreed that the police had a duty to inform a suspect of his rights. Similarly, the court held that a defendant enjoys not merely the right to hire a lawyer if he can afford one, but the right to be provided with one at government expense if he cannot. To make the right to counsel even more effective, the court subsequently ruled that a lawyer must be allowed to begin representing his client at the police station immediately after arrest.

The court also came to the conclusion that, in its disproportionate toll of the poor and of racial minorities, the death penalty amounted to 'cruel and unusual punishment'. Although capital punishment was not 'unusual' in an historical sense, the court declared in 1972, it was imposed so infrequently and arbitrarily that the few persons executed were being subjected to an extraordinary penalty. Several states have since enacted statutes which attempt to specify clear standards for meting out the death penalty, but the constitutionality of the statutes is uncertain. In the meantime, hundreds of convicts condemned under them have become a new generation of tenants on Death Row.

There are two major exceptions, however, to the general expansion of defendants' rights. In some jurisdictions, the right to a 'speedy' trial exists only if a two-year delay can be considered speedy. Judges and courtrooms sufficient to handle the criminal caseload are lacking. The protection against 'excessive' bail is relatively meaningless, moreover, because poor defendants are usually unable to raise even amounts which seem modest to the affluent. As a result, they must wait in jail during the lengthy pre-trial period, diminishing their chances of making an effective defence. So far, the court has found nothing unconstitutional about routine trial delays or a bail system that discriminates against the indigent.

Besides making many theoretical rights into practical ones, the court took steps to make them effective in both state and federal trials. Here was a classic anomaly of federalism. The bill of rights had not been explicitly addressed to the states, and in the case of *Barron v. Baltimore* (1833) the court ruled that state governments were not bound by it. As a result, federal trials were held according to one standard of due process and state trials according to another, usually less favourable to defendants.

The potential for removing this anomaly was created by the Fourteenth Amendment, one of the 'Reconstruction Amendments' enacted after the Civil War to prevent the southern states from mistreating blacks. Echoing the Fifth Amendment, the Fourteenth prohibited any *state* from depriving a person 'of life, liberty or property without due process of law'. This in itself did not immediately transform state trials, since the court generally construed 'due process' to mean merely the rudiments of procedural fairness. By the early twentieth century, however, the court began to accept the proposition that providing due process meant adhering to the specific terms of the bill of rights. One by one, the bill's provisions were 'incorporated' into the Fourteenth Amendment due process clause by judicial decision and made binding upon the states, vastly improving the status of the defendant in state courts.

The Fourteenth Amendment did more than extend the existing provisions of the bill of rights to the states; it also created a new right, that of 'equal protection of the laws'. Although intended, like the due process clause, to secure even-handed treatment of blacks in the former slave states, the equal protection clause was soon vitiated by two court rulings. In the *Civil Rights Cases* (1883), it was decided that the amendment outlawed only discriminatory action by state governments, not by private individuals. The state, in other words, could not enact a law segregating restaurants, but the restaurant owners were free to exclude blacks if they wished. The 'state action' doctrine effectively undermined the amendment, because most discrimination suffered by blacks could be classified as 'private'. Thirteen years later the equal protection clause was diluted further when the court, in *Plessy v. Ferguson*, held that states might segregate public facilities, including schools and transport, so long as blacks were provided with equal facilities. The most significant consequence of the 'separate but equal' doctrine was the development of two racially distinct school systems, from elementary school through university, in the southern states.

Together, the 'state action' and 'separate but equal' doctrines precluded any attempt by the federal government to outlaw racial discrimination – even if that were not a political impossibility in Congress – and prevented blacks from challenging discriminatory state legislation in the federal courts on constitutional grounds. Enthusiasm for 'Reconstruction' had waned anyway. The north was content to leave the blacks just where the 'states' rights' advocates would have them.

No basic change occurred in the constitutional status of blacks until the post-Second World War period, when the state action doctrine entered upon a long process of atrophy because the court began to look more carefully at the supposed distinction between public and private. More and more so-called 'private' discriminatory activities were found to involve the state sufficiently to put them within reach of the Fourteenth Amendment. The state was held responsible for discrimination when practised by a concessionary restaurant in a municipal car park, or by the officials of the state Republican and Democratic party organizations, or by the signatories of a real estate covenant excluding black residents from a neighbourhood.

Despite this, the state action doctrine still seemed to pose a barrier to direct enforcement of blacks' civil rights by federal statute. In 1968, however, the court found a way of circumventing the state action doctrine. Seeking a constitutional basis for upholding federal legislation prohibiting private discrimination, it turned to the Thirteenth Amendment, which had abolished slavery. That amendment, the court said, in *Jones v. Mayer*, empowered Congress to enact statutes to rid blacks of the 'badges and incidents' of slavery, that is, the racial discrimination which was the legacy of their ancestors' servitude. The practical outcome of the case was the resurrection of a long dormant 1866 statute, which outlawed discrimination by private individuals in the sale or rental of property – an 'open housing' law from the Reconstruction era.

Congress, however, had already gone off in another direction in search of constitutional authority for civil rights legislation. If there was one field of action in which the federal government exercised virtually unlimited discretion, it was in the regulation of interstate commerce. In 1964, Congress passed a civil rights act that prohibited segregation in all places of public accommodation, such as hotels, restaurants, and transport facilities, giving as its rationale the need to rid interstate commerce of the burden of racial discrimination. Even the most self-sufficient local restaurant bought some commodity, whether food, forks, or flypaper, that had moved in interstate commerce.

Like 'state action', the doctrine of 'separate but equal' came under more intensive judicial scrutiny in the post-war years, and the court was dissatisfied with what it saw. For the reality of 'separate but equal' contradicted the theory. Schools for blacks were not equal to white schools in either physical plant, textbooks, teacher qualifications, curriculum or funds. The judicial attack on the doctrine began at the level of graduate and professional education, since it was plainly ludicrous for the states to pretend to provide equivalent faculties and facilities for a handful of black graduate students. When Texas established a makeshift law school for blacks rather than let them enter the regular state law school, the court in 1950 noted acerbically: 'It is difficult to believe that one who had a free choice between these law schools would consider the question closed.'

Unlike state action, however, 'separate but equal' ultimately came to an abrupt end, unanimously overruled by the court in one of its most momentous cases, *Brown v. Board of Education* (1954). The justices concluded that no matter how good black schools might become in tangible qualities, 'separate educational facilities are inherently unequal' because racial segregation 'generates a feeling of inferiority' in black students.

Although *Brown* made it impossible for states to require school segregation by law, integrating the schools proved to be a perplexing problem. After two decades of often violent resistance to integration, only about half of black students in the south attend racially mixed schools. Moreover, it became clear soon after *Brown* that segregation was not a southern problem alone. That decision, in fact, put northern and southern school systems on the same footing. In both, blacks attended black schools and whites attended white schools, not because of any legal requirements but because of patterns of residential segregation. *Brown* spelled the end of *de jure* school segregation, separation by law; it did not reach *de facto* segregation, which results from having all-black and all-white neighbourhoods.

Yet if segregated education is inferior to integrated education, is it not a denial of equal protection to permit it to continue, regardless of whether it is mandated by law or perpetuated by residential segregation? With respect to the south, the court has declared that school districts which once were legally segregated have a duty to remedy the residual effects by taking positive steps to put black and white pupils into the same building. The court thus has sanctioned bussing students out of their own neighbourhoods into schools where another race predominates. With respect to the north, the court has taken the position that official policies which reinforce residential segregation, such as the drawing of attendance zones along racial lines, amount to *de jure* school segregation. Where such acts can be proved, the court has considered bussing an appropriate remedy for 'dual school systems'. In the larger metropolitan areas, however, blacks are concentrated within the city school district and the whites in separate suburban school districts. Bussing between districts offers the only possibility for achieving racial balance, but to justify it the court would have to find *de jure* segregation. And to do that would require showing either that the officials of all the districts had participated in fostering segregation or that the state government, which has overall responsibility for education, did so.

A classic case was presented to the court in 1974, involving the city of Detroit. Two thirds of the students in the city proper were black; the 'minority' group was a majority inside the city, making school integration impossible. But surrounding the city was a ring of suburbs whose schools were overwhelmingly white. A federal judge ordered bussing between city and suburban schools, but he was overruled by the Supreme Court, which held that it had not been proven that the suburban districts had followed discriminatory policies. Thus, they could not be compulsorily included in an integration scheme. The court refused to accept the theory of overall state responsibility for demographic patterns. It considered each of the suburban districts as a discrete unit and turned the city limits into a virtually impenetrable barrier to bussing. The decision seemed to mark the limit of the court's twenty-year commitment to promoting integration, since it foreclosed the only practical alternative to northern-style segregation.

Just as he has been denied equal educational opportunity, despite the Fourteenth Amendment, the black has also been kept until recently from full exercise of the suffrage despite the Fifteenth Amendment's explicit prohibition against denial of the right to vote because of 'race, colour or previous condition of servitude'. The Fifteenth Amendment, the last of the Reconstruction amendments, was intended to prevent the southern states from disenfranchising the newly freed slaves, but the states resorted to several ingenious devices to circumvent the spirit of the amendment: the literacy test, the poll tax, the 'grandfather clause' and the white primary law.

The poll tax was a registration fee for voting, usually payable a considerable time before the election. As the poorest class in the south, blacks were naturally deterred from voting by the fee requirement. Even those who could pay and were willing often found that they had missed the payment deadline, which was much less publicized than the election date. Despite its discriminatory effect, the poll tax was held constitutional by the Supreme Court in 1937, but it was abolished for all federal elections by the Twenty-fourth Amendment in 1964.

The white primary was a mechanism for denying even registered black voters any influence in the choice of candidates. In the south's one-party states, where the Democrats invariably swept the general election, the real contest took place in primary elections within the Democratic party. Under the assumption that the party was a 'private association', the Democrats excluded blacks from membership and from the privilege of voting in their primary. In the late 1940s, the Supreme Court held that a primary was an integral stage of the electoral process and that parties were sufficiently imbued with official sanction for their discriminatory acts to be construed as 'state action'. Attempts by the Democrats to evade the issue by holding unofficial pre-primary elections were subsequently invalidated as well by the court.

Grandfather clauses typically stipulated that anyone whose ancestors did not have the right to vote in 1860, the year before the Civil War began, must pass a literacy test to qualify for the franchise. Illiterate whites, however, were free to vote. The grandfather clause was invalidated by the Supreme Court in 1915, but the literacy test remained. If a state wished to require a literacy test, it had to require all registrants, regardless of their ancestry, to pass it. However, the test was usually administered in a discriminatory fashion by the registrars. A common test as late as the 1960s asked blacks to read and 'interpret' sections of the constitution; the applicant's interpretation was then declared 'wrong'.

The literacy test remained a formidable barrier to black participation in politics until Congress passed the Voting Rights Act of 1965, under its power to enforce the Fifteenth Amendment. The act authorized federally appointed registrars to be substituted for state registrars in places where only a small proportion of blacks were enrolled voters. Since then, more than half of the south's six million blacks of voting age have registered, making the blacks in most southern states a sizable minority voting bloc that often can decide the fate of elections. Even formerly staunch segregationists like Governor George Wallace of Alabama have been forced to woo black voters with more moderate utterances. The Voting Rights Act has also cleared the way for blacks to be elected to public office. Before the act, less than 100 blacks held elective offices in the southern states, but by 1974 the number had risen to almost 1400. Black officeholding is still disproportionately small, however. In more than a third of the southern counties where blacks are a majority of the population there is not a single black official.

Blacks are only one of the minority groups which have been able to redress their weak position in the political arena by relying upon the rights guaranteed by the constitution. Various dissident political and religious groups, *avant-garde* cultural movements and other isolated minorities have also successfully leaned on them to withstand the majority's pressures towards conformity. By association with such pariahs, constitutional rights often tend to be disparaged in practice. That is, the average person, if asked, might say that he supports the First Amendment and freedom of speech but is opposed to Nazis being allowed to hold a public rally. There is, indeed, good reason to believe that the bill of rights would not pass today if put to a referendum under another name. Fortunately, however, the bill of rights has been invested with the same reverence as the rest of the constitution so that its provisions, no matter how annoying when invoked, have taken on the glow of hallowed tradition. No better security for civil liberties could be imagined.

Constitution of the United States of America

We the people of the United States, in Order to form a more perfect Union, establish Justice, insure domestic Tranquility, provide for the common defence, promote the general Welfare, and secure the Blessings of Liberty to ourselves and our Posterity, do ordain and establish this CONSTITUTION for the United States of America.

ARTICLE I

SECTION 1. All legislative Powers herein granted shall be vested in a Congress of the United States, which shall consist of a Senate and House of Representatives.

SECTION 2. (1) The House of Representatives shall be composed of Members chosen every second Year by the People of the several States, and the Electors in each State shall have the Qualifications requisite for Electors of the most numerous Branch of the State Legislature.

(2) No person shall be a Representative who shall not have attained to the Age of twenty five Years, and been seven Years a Citizen of the United States, and who shall not, when elected, be an inhabitant of that State in which he shall be chosen.

(3) Representatives and direct Taxes shall be apportioned among the several States which may be included within this Union according to their respective Numbers, which shall be determined by adding to the whole Number of free Persons, including those bound to Service for a Term of Years, and excluding Indians not taxed, three fifths of all other Persons. The actual Enumeration shall be made within three Years

after the first Meeting of the Congress of the United States, and within every subsequent Term of ten Years, in such Manner as they shall by Law direct. The Number of Representatives shall not exceed one for every thirty Thousand, but each State shall have at least one Representative; and until such enumeration shall be made, the State of New Hampshire shall be entitled to chuse three, Massachusetts eight, Rhode-Island and Providence Plantations one, Connecticut five, New-York six, New Jersey four, Pennsylvania eight, Delaware one, Maryland six, Virginia ten, North Carolina five, South Carolina five, and Georgia three.

(4) When vacancies happen in the Representation from any State, the Executive Authority thereof shall issue Writs of Election to fill such Vacancies.

(5) The House of Representatives shall chuse their Speaker and other Officers; and shall have the sole Power of Impeachment.

SECTION 3. (1) The Senate of the United States shall be composed of two Senators from each State, chosen by the Legislature thereof, for six Years; and each Senator shall have one Vote.

(2) Immediately after they shall be assembled in Consequence of the first Election, they shall be divided as equally as may be into three Classes. The Seats of the Senators of the first Class shall be vacated at the Expiration of the second Year, of the second Class at the Expiration of the fourth Year, and of the third Class at the Expiration of the sixth Year, so that one third may be chosen every second Year; and if Vacancies happen by Resignation, or otherwise, during the Recess of the Legislature of any State, the Executive thereof may make temporary Appointments until the next Meeting of the Legislature, which shall then fill such Vacancies.

(3) No Person shall be a Senator who shall not have attained to the Age of thirty Years, and been nine Years a Citizen of the United States, and who shall not, when elected, be an inhabitant of that State for which he shall be chosen.

(4) The Vice President of the United States shall be President of the Senate, but shall have no Vote, unless they be equally divided.

(5) The Senate shall chuse their other Officers, and also a President pro tempore, in the Absence of the Vice President, or when he shall exercise the Office of President of the United States.

(6) The Senate shall have the sole Power to try all Impeachments. When sitting for that Purpose, they shall be on Oath or Affirmation. When the President of the United States is tried, the Chief Justice shall preside: And no Person shall be convicted without the Concurrence of two thirds of the Members present.

(7) Judgment in Cases of Impeachment shall not extend further than to removal from office, and disqualification to hold and enjoy any Office of honor, Trust or Profit under the United States: but the Party convicted shall nevertheless be liable and subject to Indictment, Trial, Judgment and Punishment, according to Law.

SECTION 4. (1) The Times, Places and Manner of holding Elections for Senators and Representatives, shall be prescribed in each State by the Legislature thereof; but the Congress may at any time by Law make or alter such Regulations, except as to the Places of chusing Senators.

(2) The Congress shall assemble at least once in every Year, and such Meeting shall be on the first Monday in December, unless they shall by Law appoint a different Day.

SECTION 5. (1) Each House shall be the Judge of the Elections, Returns and Qualifications of its own Members, and a Majority of each shall constitute a Quorum to do Business; but a smaller Number may adjourn from day to day, and may be authorized to compel the attendance of absent Members, in such Manner, and under such Penalties as each House may provide.

(2) Each House may determine the Rules of its Proceedings,

punish its Members for Disorderly Behaviour, and, with the Concurrence of two thirds, expel a Member.

(3) Each House shall keep a Journal of its Proceedings, and from time to time publish the same, excepting such Parts as may in their Judgment require Secrecy; and the Yeas and Nays of the Members of either House on any question shall, at the Desire of one fifth of those Present, be entered on the Journal.

(4) Neither House, during the Session of Congress, shall, without the Consent of the other, adjourn for more than three days, nor to any other Place than that in which the two Houses shall be sitting.

SECTION 6. (1) The Senators and Representatives shall receive a Compensation for their Services, to be ascertained by Law, and paid out of the Treasury of the United States. They shall in all Cases, except Treason, Felony and Breach of the Peace, be privileged from Arrest during their Attendance at the Session of their respective Houses, and in going to and returning from the same; and for any Speech or Debate in either House, they shall not be questioned in any other Place.

(2) No Senator or Representative shall, during the Time for which he was elected, be appointed to any civil Office under the Authority of the United States, which shall have been created, or the Emoluments whereof shall have been encreased during such time; and no Person holding any Office under the United States, shall be a member of either House during his Continuance in Office.

SECTION 7. (1) All Bills for raising Revenue shall originate in the House of Representatives; but the Senate may propose or concur with Amendments as on other Bills.

(2) Every Bill which shall have passed the House of Representatives and the Senate, shall, before it become a Law, be presented to the President of the United States; if he approve he shall sign it, but if not he shall return it, with his

Objections to that House in which it shall have originated, who shall enter the Objections at large on their Journal, and proceed to reconsider it. If after such Reconsideration two thirds of that House shall agree to pass the Bill, it shall be sent, together with the Objections, to the other House, by which it shall likewise be reconsidered, and if approved by two thirds of that House, it shall become a Law. But in all such Cases the Votes of both Houses shall be determined by yeas and Nays, and the Names of the Persons voting for and against the Bill shall be entered on the Journal of each House respectively. If any Bill shall not be returned by the President within ten Days (Sundays excepted) after it shall have been presented to him, the same shall be a Law, in like Manner as if he had signed it, unless the Congress by their Adjournment prevent its Return, in which Case it shall not be a Law.

(3) Every Order, Resolution, or Vote to which the Concurrence of the Senate and House of Representatives may be necessary (except on a question of Adjournment) shall be presented to the President of the United States; and before the same shall take Effect, shall be approved by him, or being disapproved by him, shall be repassed by two thirds of the Senate and House of Representatives, according to the Rules and Limitations prescribed in the Case of a Bill.

SECTION 8. The Congress shall have Power (1) to lay and collect Taxes, Duties, Imposts and Excises, to pay the Debts and provide for the common Defence and general Welfare of the United States; but all Duties, Imposts and Excises shall be uniform throughout the United States;

(2) To borrow Money on the credit of the United States;

(3) To regulate Commerce with foreign Nations, and among the several States, and with the Indian Tribes;

(4) To establish an uniform Rule of Naturalization, and uniform Laws on the subject of Bankruptcies throughout the United States;

(5) To coin Money, regulate the Value thereof, and of foreign Coin, and fix the Standard of Weights and Measures;

(6) To provide for the Punishment of counterfeiting the Securities and current Coin of the United States;

(7) To establish Post Offices and post Roads;

(8) To promote the Progress of Science and useful Arts, by securing for limited Times to Authors and Inventors the exclusive Right to their respective Writings and Discoveries;

(9) To constitute Tribunals inferior to the supreme Court;

(10) To define and punish Piracies and Felonies committed on the high Seas, and Offences against the Law of Nations;

(11) To declare War, grant Letters of Marque and Reprisal, and make Rules concerning Captures on Land and Water;

(12) To raise and support Armies, but no Appropriation of Money to that Use shall be for a longer Term than two Years;

(13) To provide and maintain a Navy;

(14) To make Rules for the Government and Regulation of the land and naval Forces;

(15) To provide for calling forth the Militia to execute the Laws of the Union, suppress Insurrections and repel invasions;

(16) To provide for organizing, arming, and disciplining, the Militia, and for governing such Part of them as may be employed in the Service of the United States, reserving to the States respectively, the Appointment of the Officers, and the Authority of training the Militia according to the discipline prescribed by Congress;

(17) To exercise exclusive Legislation in all Cases whatsoever, over such District (not exceeding ten Miles square) as may, by Cession of particular States, and the Acceptance of Congress, become the Seat of the Government of the United States, and to exercise like Authority over all Places purchased by the Consent of the Legislature of the State in which the same shall be, for the Erection of Forts, Magazines, Arsenals, dock-Yards, and other needful Buildings; – And

(18) To make all Laws which shall be necessary and proper for carrying into Execution the foregoing Powers, and all other Powers vested by this Constitution in the Government of the United States, or in any Department or Officer thereof.

SECTION 9. (1) The Migration or Importation of such Persons as any of the States now existing shall think proper to admit, shall not be prohibited by the Congress prior to the Year one thousand eight hundred and eight, but a Tax or duty may be imposed on such Importation, not exceeding ten dollars for each Person.

(2) The Privilege of the Writ of Habeas Corpus shall not be suspended, unless when in Cases of Rebellion or Invasion the public Safety may require it.

(3) No Bill of Attainder or ex post facto Law shall be passed.

(4) No Capitation, or other direct, Tax shall be laid, unless in Proportion to the Census or Enumeration herein before directed to be taken.

(5) No Tax or Duty shall be laid on Articles exported from any State.

(6) No Preference shall be given by any Regulation of Commerce or Revenue to the Ports of one State over those of another: nor shall Vessels bound to, or from, one State, be obliged to enter, clear, or pay Duties in another.

(7) No Money shall be drawn from the Treasury, but in Consequence of Appropriations made by Law; and a regular Statement and Account of the Receipts and Expenditures of all public Money shall be published from time to time.

(8) No Title of Nobility shall be granted by the United States: And no Person holding any Office of Profit or Trust under them, shall, without the Consent of the Congress, accept of any present, Emolument, Office, or Title, of any kind whatever, from any King, Prince, or foreign State.

SECTION 10. (1) No State shall enter into any Treaty, Alliance, or Confederation; grant Letters of Marque and Reprisal; coin Money; emit Bills of Credit; make any Thing but gold and silver Coin a Tender in Payment of Debts; pass any Bill of Attainder, ex post facto Law, or Law impairing the Obligation of Contracts, or grant any Title of Nobility.

(2) No State shall, without the Consent of the Congress,

lay any Imposts or Duties on Imports or Exports, except what may be absolutely necessary for executing its inspection Laws; and the net Produce of all Duties and Imposts, laid by any State on Imports or Exports, shall be for the Use of the Treasury of the United States; and all such Laws shall be subject to the Revision and Control of the Congress.

(3) No State shall, without the Consent of Congress, lay any Duty of Tonnage, keep Troops, or Ships of War in time of Peace, enter into any Agreement or Compact with another State, or with a foreign Power, or engage in War, unless actually invaded, or in such imminent Danger as will not admit of delay.

ARTICLE II

SECTION I. (1) The executive Power shall be vested in a President of the United States of America. He shall hold his office during the Term of four Years, and, together with the Vice President, chosen for the same Term, be elected, as follows.

(2) Each State shall appoint, in such Manner as the Legislature thereof may direct, a Number of Electors, equal to the whole Number of Senators and Representatives to which the State may be entitled in the Congress: but no Senator or Representative, or Person holding an Office of Trust or Profit under the United States, shall be appointed an Elector.

(3) The Electors shall meet in their respective States, and vote by Ballot for two Persons, of whom one at least shall not be an inhabitant of the same State with themselves. And they shall make a List of all the Persons voted for, and of the Number of Votes for each; which List they shall sign and certify, and transmit sealed to the Seat of Government of the United States, directed to the President of the Senate. The President of the Senate shall, in the Presence of the Senate and House of Representatives, open all the Certificates, and the Votes shall then be counted. The Person having the

greatest Number of Votes shall be the President, if such Number be a Majority of the whole Number of Electors appointed; and if there be more than one who have such Majority, and have an equal Number of Votes, then the House of Representatives shall immediately chuse by Ballot one of them for President; and if no Person have a Majority, then from the five highest on the List the said House shall in like Manner chuse the President. But in chusing the President, the Votes shall be taken by States, the Representation from each State having one Vote; A quorum for this Purpose shall consist of a Member or Members from two thirds of the States, and a Majority of all the States shall be necessary to a Choice. In every Case, after the Choice of the President, the Person having the greatest Number of Votes of the Electors shall be the Vice President. But if there should remain two or more who have equal Votes, the Senate shall chuse from them by Ballot the Vice President.

(4) The Congress may determine the Time of chusing the Electors, and the Day on which they shall give their Votes; which Day shall be the same throughout the United States.

(5) No Person except a natural born Citizen, or a Citizen of the United States, at the time of the Adoption of this Constitution, shall be eligible to the Office of President; neither shall any Person be eligible to that Office who shall not have attained to the Age of thirty five Years, and been fourteen Years a Resident within the United States.

(6) In Case of the Removal of the President from Office, or of his Death, Resignation, or Inability to discharge the Powers and Duties of the said Office, the Same shall devolve on the Vice President, and the Congress may by Law provide for the Case of Removal, Death, Resignation, or Inability, both of the President and Vice President, declaring what officer shall then act as President, and such Officer shall act accordingly, until the Disability be removed, or a President shall be elected.

(7) The President shall, at stated Times, receive for his Services, a Compensation, which shall neither be encreased

nor diminished during the Period for which he shall have been elected, and he shall not receive within that Period any other Emolument from the United States, or any of them.

(8) Before he enter on the Execution of his Office, he shall take the following Oath or Affirmation: – 'I do solemnly swear (or affirm) that I will faithfully execute the Office of President of the United States, and will to the best of my Ability, preserve, protect and defend the Constitution of the United States.'

SECTION 2. (1) The President shall be Commander in Chief of the Army and Navy of the United States, and of the Militia of the several States, when called into the actual Service of the United States; he may require the Opinion, in writing, of the principal Officer in each of the executive Departments, upon any Subject relating to the Duties of their respective Offices, and he shall have Power to grant Reprieves and Pardons for Offences against the United States, except in Cases of Impeachment.

(2) He shall have Power, by and with the Advice and Consent of the Senate, to make Treaties, provided two thirds of the Senators present concur; and he shall nominate, and by and with the Advice and Consent of the Senate, shall appoint Ambassadors, other public Ministers and Consuls, Judges of the supreme Court, and all other Officers of the United States, whose Appointments are not herein otherwise provided for, and which shall be established by Law: but the Congress may by law vest the Appointment of such inferior Officers, as they think proper, in the President alone, in the Courts of Law, or in the Heads of Departments.

(3) The President shall have Power to fill up all Vacancies that may happen during the Recess of the Senate, by granting Commissions which shall expire at the End of their next Session.

SECTION 3. He shall from time to time give to the Congress Information of the State of the Union, and recommend to their Consideration such Measures as he shall judge necessary and expedient; he may, on extraordinary Occasions, convene both Houses, or either of them, and in Case of Disagreement between them, with Respect to the Time of Adjournment, he may adjourn them to such Time as he shall think proper; he shall receive Ambassadors and other public Ministers; he shall take Care that the Laws be faithfully executed, and shall Commission all the Officers of the United States.

SECTION 4. The President, Vice President and all civil Officers of the United States, shall be removed from Office on Impeachment for, and Conviction of, Treason, Bribery, or other high Crimes and Misdemeanors.

ARTICLE III

SECTION 1. The Judicial Power of the United States, shall be vested in one supreme Court, and in such inferior Courts as the Congress may from time to time ordain and establish. The Judges, both of the supreme and inferior Courts, shall hold their Offices during good Behaviour, and shall, at stated Times, receive for their Services, a Compensation, which shall not be diminished during their Continuance in Office.

SECTION 2. (1) The Judicial Power shall extend to all Cases, in Law and Equity, arising under this Constitution, the Laws of the United States, and Treaties made, or which shall be made, under their Authority; – to all Cases affecting Ambassadors, other public Ministers and Consuls; – to all Cases of admiralty and maritime Jurisdiction; – to Controversies to which the United States shall be a Party; – to Controversies between two or more States; – between a State and Citizens of another State; – between Citizens of different States; – between Citizens of the same State claiming Lands under Grants of different States, and between a State, or the Citizens thereof, and foreign States, Citizens or Subjects.

(2) In all Cases affecting Ambassadors, other public

Ministers and Consuls, and those in which a State shall be Party, the supreme Court shall have original Jurisdiction. In all the other Cases before mentioned, the Supreme Court shall have appellate Jurisdiction, both as to Law and Fact, with such Exceptions, and under such Regulations as the Congress shall make.

(3) The Trial of all Crimes, except in Cases of impeachment, shall be by Jury; and such Trial shall be held in the State where the said Crimes shall have been committed; but when not committed within any State, the Trial shall be at such Place or Places as the Congress may by Law have directed.

SECTION 3. (1) Treason against the United States, shall consist only in levying War against them, or in adhering to their Enemies, giving them Aid and Comfort. No Person shall be convicted of Treason unless on the Testimony of two Witnesses to the same overt Act, or on Confession in open Court.

(2) The Congress shall have Power to declare the Punishment of Treason, but no Attainder of Treason shall work Corruption of Blood, or Forfeiture except during the Life of the Person attained.

ARTICLE IV

SECTION 1. Full Faith and Credit shall be given in each State to the public Acts, Records, and judicial Proceedings of every other State. And the Congress may by general Laws prescribe the Manner in which such Acts, Records and Proceedings shall be proved, and the Effect thereof.

SECTION 2. (1) The Citizens of each State shall be entitled to all Privileges and Immunities of Citizens in the several States.

(2) A Person charged in any State with Treason, Felony, or other Crime, who shall flee from Justice, and be found in

another State, shall on Demand of the executive Authority of the State from which he fled, be delivered up, to be removed to the State having Jurisdiction of the Crime.

(3) No Person held to Service or Labour in one State, under the Laws thereof, escaping into another, shall, in Consequence of any Law or Regulation therein, be discharged from such Service or Labour, but shall be delivered up on Claim of the Party to whom such Service or Labour may be due.

SECTION 3. (1) New States may be admitted by the Congress into this Union; but no new State shall be formed or erected within the Jurisdiction of any other States; nor any State be formed by the Junction of two or more States, or Parts of States, without the Consent of the Legislatures of the States concerned as well as of the Congress.

(2) The Congress shall have Power to dispose of and make all needful Rules and Regulations respecting the Territory or other Property belonging to the United States; and nothing in this Constitution shall be so construed as to Prejudice any Claims of the United States, or of any particular State.

SECTION 4. The United States shall guarantee to every State in this Union a Republican Form of Government, and shall protect each of them against Invasion; and on Application of the Legislature, or of the Executive (when the Legislature cannot be convened) against domestic Violence.

ARTICLE V

The Congress, whenever two thirds of both Houses shall deem it necessary, shall propose Amendments to this Constitution, or, on the Application of the Legislatures of two thirds of the several States, shall call a Convention for proposing Amendments, which, in either Case, shall be valid to all Intents and Purposes, as Part of this Constitution, when ratified by the Legislatures of three fourths of the several States, or by Conventions in three fourths thereof, as the one or the other Mode of Ratification may be proposed by the Congress; Provided that no Amendment which may be made prior to the Year One thousand eight hundred and eight shall in any Manner affect the first and fourth Clauses in the Ninth Section of the first Article; and that no State, without its Consent, shall be deprived of its equal Suffrage in the Senate.

ARTICLE VI

(1) All Debts contracted and Engagements entered into, before the Adoption of this Constitution, shall be as valid against the United States under this Constitution, as under the Confederation.

(2) This Constitution, and the Laws of the United States which shall be made in Pursuance thereof; and all Treaties made, or which shall be made, under the Authority of the United States, shall be the supreme Law of the Land; and the Judges in every State shall be bound thereby, any Thing in the Constitution or Laws of any State to the Contrary notwithstanding.

(3) The Senators and Representatives before mentioned, and the Members of the several State Legislatures, and all executive and judicial Officers, both of the United States and of the several States, shall be bound by Oath or affirmation, to support this Constitution; but no religious Test shall ever be required as a Qualification to any Office or Public Trust under the United States.

ARTICLE VII

The Ratification of the Conventions of nine States, shall be sufficient for the Establishment of this Constitution between the States so ratifying the Same.

Amendments

AMENDMENT I

Congress shall make no law respecting an establishment of religion, or prohibiting the free exercise thereof; or abridging the freedom of speech, or of the press; or the right of the people peaceably to assemble, and to petition the Government for a redress of grievances.

AMENDMENT II

A well regulated Militia, being necessary to the security of a free State, the right of the people to keep and bear Arms, shall not be infringed.

AMENDMENT III

No Soldier shall, in time of peace be quartered in any house, without the consent of the Owner, nor in time of war, but in a manner to be prescribed by law.

AMENDMENT IV

The right of the people to be secure in their persons, houses, papers, and effects, against unreasonable searches and seizures, shall not be violated, and no Warrants shall issue, but upon probable cause, supported by Oath or affirmation, and particularly describing the place to be searched, and the persons or things to be seized.

AMENDMENT V

No person shall be held to answer for a capital, or otherwise infamous crime, unless on a presentment or indictment of a Grand Jury, except in cases arising in the land or naval forces, or in the Militia, when in actual service in time of War or public danger; nor shall any person be subject for the same offence to be twice put in jeopardy of life or limb; nor shall be compelled in any criminal case to be a witness against himself; nor be deprived of life, liberty, or property, without due process of law; nor shall private property be taken for public use, without just compensation.

AMENDMENT VI

In all criminal prosecutions the accused shall enjoy the right to a speedy and public trial, by an impartial jury of the State and district wherein the crime shall have been committed, which district shall have been previously ascertained by law, and to be informed of the nature and cause of the accusation; to be confronted with the witnesses against him; to have compulsory process for obtaining witnesses in his favor, and to have the Assistance of Counsel for his defence.

AMENDMENT VII

In suits at common law, where the value in controversy shall exceed twenty dollars, the right of trial by jury shall be preserved, and no fact tried by a jury shall be otherwise re-examined in any Court of the United States, than according to the rules of the common law.

AMENDMENT VIII

Excessive bail shall not be required, nor excessive fines imposed, nor cruel and unusual punishments inflicted.

AMENDMENT IX

The enumeration in the Constitution, of certain rights, shall not be construed to deny or disparage others retained by the people.

AMENDMENT X

The powers not delegated to the United States by the Constitution, nor prohibited by it to the States, are reserved to the States respectively, or to the people.

[The first ten Amendments, known as the Bill of Rights, were adopted in 1791.]

AMENDMENT XI

The Judicial power of the United States shall not be construed to extend to any suit in law or equity, commenced or prosecuted against one of the United States by Citizens of another State, or by Citizens or Subjects of any Foreign State. [1798]

AMENDMENT XII

The Electors shall meet in their respective states, and vote by ballot for President and Vice President, one of whom, at least, shall not be an inhabitant of the same state with themselves; they shall name in their ballots the person voted for as President, and in distinct ballots the person voted for as Vice President, and they shall make distinct lists of all persons voted for as President, and of all persons voted for as Vice President, and of the number of votes for each, which lists they shall sign and certify, and transmit sealed to the seat of the government of the United States, directed to the President of the Senate; – The President of the Senate shall, in the presence of the Senate and House of Representatives, open all the certificates and the votes shall then be counted; – The person having the greatest number of votes for President, shall be the President, if such number be a majority of the whole number of Electors appointed; and if no person have such majority, then from the persons having the highest numbers not exceeding three on the list of those voted for as President, the House of Representatives shall choose immediately, by ballot, the President. But in choosing the President, the votes shall be taken by states, the representation from each state having one vote; a quorum for this purpose shall consist of a member or members from two thirds of the states, and a majority of all the states shall be necessary to a choice. And if the House of Representatives shall not choose a President whenever the right of choice shall devolve upon them, before the fourth day of March next following, then the Vice President shall act as President, as in the case of the death or other constitutional disability of the President. – The person having the greatest number of votes as Vice President, shall be the Vice President, if such number be a majority of the whole number of Electors appointed, and if no person have a majority, then from the two highest numbers on the list, the Senate shall choose the Vice President; a quorum for the purpose shall consist of two thirds of the whole number of Senators, and a majority of the whole number shall be necessary to a choice. But no person constitutionally ineligible to the office of President shall be eligible to that of Vice President of the United States. [1804]

AMENDMENT XIII

SECTION 1. Neither slavery nor involuntary servitude, except as a punishment for crime whereof the party shall have been duly convicted, shall exist within the United States, or any place subject to their jurisdiction.

SECTION 2. Congress shall have power to enforce this article by appropriate legislation. [1865]

AMENDMENT XIV

SECTION 1. All persons born or naturalized in the United States, and subject to the jurisdiction thereof, are citizens of the United States and of the State wherein they reside. No State shall make or enforce any law which shall abridge the privileges or immunities of citizens of the United States; nor shall any State deprive any person of life, liberty, or property, without due process of law; nor deny to any person within its jurisdiction the equal protection of the laws.

SECTION 2. Representatives shall be apportioned among the several States according to their respective numbers, counting the whole number of persons in each State, excluding Indians not taxed. But when the right to vote at any election for the choice of electors for President and Vice President of the United States, Representatives in Congress, the Executive and Judicial officers of a State, or the members of the Legislature thereof, is denied to any of the male inhabitants of such State, being twenty-one years of age, and citizens of the United States, or in any way abridged, except for participation in rebellion, or other crime, the basis of representation therein shall be reduced in the proportion which the number of such male citizens shall bear to the whole number of male citizens twenty-one years of age in such State.

SECTION 3. No person shall be a Senator or Representative in Congress, or elector of President and Vice President, or hold any office, civil or military, under the United States, or under any State, who, having previously taken an oath, as a member of Congress, or as an officer of the United States, or as a member of any State legislature, or as an executive or judicial officer of any State, to support the Constitution of the United States, shall have engaged in insurrection or rebellion against the same, or given aid or comfort to the enemies thereof. But Congress may by a vote of two thirds of each House, remove such disability.

SECTION 4. The validity of the public debt of the United States, authorized by law, including debts incurred for payment of pensions and bounties for services in suppressing insurrection or rebellion, shall not be questioned. But neither the United States nor any State shall assume or pay any debt or obligation incurred in aid of insurrection or rebellion

against the United States, or any claim for the loss or eman-
cipation of any slave; but all such debts, obligations and
claims shall be held illegal and void.

SECTION 5. The Congress shall have power to enforce, by
appropriate legislation, the provisions of this article. [1868]

AMENDMENT XV

SECTION 1. The right of citizens of the United States to
vote shall not be denied or abridged by the United States or
by any State on account of race, color, or previous condition
of servitude.

SECTION 2. The Congress shall have power to enforce this
article by appropriate legislation. [1870]

AMENDMENT XVI

The Congress shall have power to lay and collect taxes on
incomes, from whatever source derived, without apportionment
among the several States, and without regard to any census or
enumeration. [1913]

AMENDMENT XVII

The Senate of the United States shall be composed of two
Senators from each State, elected by the people thereof, for
six years; and each Senator shall have one vote. The electors
in each State shall have the qualifications requisite for electors
of the most numerous branch of the State legislatures.

When vacancies happen in the representation of any State
in the Senate, the executive authority of such State shall issue
writs of election to fill such vacancies: *Provided*, That the
legislature of any State may empower the executive thereof
to make temporary appointments until the people fill the
vacancies by election as the legislature may direct.

This amendment shall not be so construed as to affect the election or term of any Senator chosen before it becomes valid as part of the Constitution. [1913]

AMENDMENT XVIII

SECTION 1. After one year from the ratification of this article the manufacture, sale, or transportation of intoxicating liquors within, the importation thereof into, or the exportation thereof from the United States and all territory subject to the jurisdiction thereof for beverage purposes is hereby prohibited.

SECTION 2. The Congress and the several States shall have concurrent power to enforce this article by appropriate legislation.

SECTION 3. This article shall be inoperative unless it shall have been ratified as an amendment to the Constitution by the legislatures of the several States, as provided in the Constitution, within seven years from the date of the submission hereof to the States by the Congress. [1919]

AMENDMENT XIX

The right of citizens of the United States to vote shall not be denied or abridged by the United States or by any State on account of sex.

Congress shall have power to enforce this article by appropriate legislation. [1920]

AMENDMENT XX

SECTION 1. The terms of the President and Vice President shall end at noon at the 20th day of January, and the terms of Senators and Representatives at noon on the 3rd day of January, of the years in which such terms would have ended if this article had not been ratified; and the terms of their successors shall then begin.

SECTION 2. The Congress shall assemble at least once in every year, and such meeting shall begin at noon on the 3rd day of January, unless they shall by law appoint a different day.

SECTION 3. If, at the time fixed for the beginning of the term of the President, the President elect shall have died, the Vice President elect shall become President. If a President shall not have been chosen before the time fixed for the beginning of his term, or if the President elect shall have failed to qualify, then the Vice President elect shall act as President until a President shall have qualified; and the Congress may by law provide for the case wherein neither a President elect nor a Vice President elect shall have qualified, declaring who shall then act as President, or the manner in which one who is to act shall be selected, and such person shall act accordingly until a President or Vice President shall have qualified.

SECTION 4. The Congress may by law provide for the case of the death of any of the persons from whom the House of Representatives may choose a President whenever the right of choice shall have devolved upon them, and for the case of the death of any of the persons from whom the Senate may choose a Vice President whenever the right of choice shall have devolved upon them.

SECTION 5. Sections 1 and 2 shall take effect on the 15th day of October following the ratification of this article.

SECTION 6. This article shall be inoperative unless it shall have been ratified as an amendment to the Constitution by the legislatures of three fourths of the several States within seven years from the date of its submission. [1933]

AMENDMENT XXI

SECTION 1. The eighteenth article of amendment to the Constitution of the United States is hereby repealed.

SECTION 2. The transportation or importation into any State, Territory, or possession of the United States for delivery or use therein of intoxicating liquors, in violation of the laws thereof, is hereby prohibited.

SECTION 3. This article shall be inoperative unless it shall have been ratified as an amendment to the Constitution by conventions in the several States, as provided in the Constitution, within seven years from the date of the submission hereof to the States by the Congress. [1933]

AMENDMENT XXII

SECTION 1. No person shall be elected to the office of the President more than twice, and no person who has held the office of President, or acted as President, for more than two years of a term to which some other person was elected President shall be elected to the office of the President more than once. But this Article shall not apply to any persons holding the office of President when this Article was proposed by the Congress, and shall not prevent any person who may be holding the office of President, or acting as President, during the term within which this Article becomes operative from holding the office of President or acting as President during the remainder of such term.

SECTION 2. This Article shall be inoperative unless it shall have been ratified as an amendment to the Constitution by the legislatures of three fourths of the several States within seven years from the date of its submission to the states by the Congress. [1951]

AMENDMENT XXIII

SECTION 1. The District constituting the seat of Government of the United States shall appoint in such manner as the Congress may direct:

A number of electors of President and Vice President equal to the whole number of Senators and Representatives in Congress to which the District would be entitled if it were a State, but in no event more than the least populous states; they shall be in addition to those appointed by the States, but they shall be considered, for the purposes of the election of President and Vice President, to be electors appointed by a State; and they shall meet in the District and perform such duties as provided by the twelfth article of amendment.

SECTION 2. The Congress shall have power to enforce this article by appropriate legislation. [1961]

AMENDMENT XXIV

SECTION 1. The right of citizens of the United States to vote in any primary or other election for President or Vice President, for electors for President or Vice President, or for Senator or Representative in Congress, shall not be denied or abridged by the United States or any State by reason of failure to pay poll tax or other tax.

SECTION 2. The Congress shall have power to enforce this article by appropriate legislation. [1964]

AMENDMENT XXV

SECTION 1. In case of the removal of the President from office or of his death or resignation, the Vice President shall become President.

SECTION 2. Whenever there is a vacancy in the office of the

Vice President, the President shall nominate a Vice President who shall take office upon confirmation by a majority vote of both Houses of Congress.

SECTION 3. Whenever the President transmits to the President pro tempore of the Senate and the Speaker of the House of Representatives his written declaration that he is unable to discharge the powers and duties of his office, and until he transmits to them a written declaration to the contrary, such powers and duties shall be discharged by the Vice President as Acting President.

SECTION 4. Whenever the Vice President and a majority of either the principal officers of the executive departments or of such other body as Congress may by law provide, transmit to the President pro tempore of the Senate and the Speaker of the House of Representatives their written declaration that the President is unable to discharge the powers and duties of his office, the Vice President shall immediately assume the powers and duties of the office as Acting President.

Thereafter, when the President transmits to the President pro tempore of the Senate and the Speaker of the House of Representatives his written declaration that no inability exists, he shall resume the powers and duties of his office unless the Vice President and a majority of either the principal officers of the executive departments or of such other body as Congress may by law provide, transmit within four days to the President pro tempore of the Senate and the Speaker of the House of Representatives their written declaration that the President is unable to discharge the powers and duties of his office. Thereupon Congress shall decide the issue, assembling within forty-eight hours for that purpose if not in session. If the Congress, within twenty-one days after receipt of the latter written declaration, or if Congress is not in session, within twenty-one days after Congress is required to assemble, determines by two thirds vote of both Houses that the President is unable to discharge the powers and duties of his office, the Vice President shall continue to discharge the same as Acting President; otherwise, the President shall resume the powers and duties of his office. [1967]

AMENDMENT XXVI

SECTION 1. The right of citizens of the United States, who are eighteen years of age or older, to vote shall not be denied or abridged by the United States or by any State on account of age.

SECTION 2. The Congress shall have the power to enforce this article by appropriate legislation. [1971]

AMENDMENT XXVII [ratification pending]

SECTION 1. Equality of rights under law shall not be denied or abridged by the United States or any State on account of sex.

SECTION 2. The Congress shall have the power to enforce by appropriate legislation the provisions of this article.

SECTION 3. This Amendment shall take effect two years after the date of ratification.

Suggestions for Further Reading

BERNARD BAILYN, *The Origins of American Politics*, 1968.

CARL BECKER, *The Declaration of Independence*, 1922.

JAMES BRYCE, *The American Commonwealth*, 1888.

JAMES BURNHAM, *Congress and the American Tradition*, 1959.

JAMES MCGREGOR BURNS, *Deadlock of Democracy*, 1963.

ANGUS CAMPBELL, *et al.*, *The American Voter*, 1960.

EDWARD S. CORWIN, *The Constitution and What It Means Today* (13th ed.), 1973.

Federalist Papers (New English Library ed.), 1961.

RICHARD HOFSTADTER, *The American Political Tradition*, 1948.

RALPH K. HUITT and ROBERT L. PEABODY, *Congress: Two Decades of Analysis*, 1967.

ALFRED H. KELLEY and WINFRED A. HARBISON, *The American Constitution: Its Origin and Development* (4th ed.), 1970.

V. O. KEY, *Public Opinion and American Democracy*, 1961.

ROBERT G. MCCLOSKEY, *The American Supreme Court*, 1960.

CHARLES H. MCILWAIN, *Constitutionalism: Ancient and Modern*, 1947.

CLINTON ROSSITER, *The American Presidency* (rev. ed.), 1970.

ALEXIS DE TOCQUEVILLE, *Democracy in America*, 1835.

THEODORE H. WHITE, *The Making of the President, 1960*, 1961.

Index

Fontana Politics

Fontana History of Europe

Praised by academics, teachers and general readers alike, this series aims to provide an account, based on the latest research, that combines narrative and explanation. Each volume has been specifically commissioned from a leading English, American or European scholar, and is complete in itself.

The general editor of the series in J. H. Plumb, lately Professor of Modern History at Cambridge University, and Fellow of Christ's College, Cambridge.

A Fontana Selection

The Sunday Gardener *(illus.)*, edited by Alan Gemmell
Ideology in Social Science, edited by Robin Blackburn
Hitler: The Führer and the People, J. P. Stern
Memories, Dreams, Reflections, C. G. Jung
The Screwtape Letters, C. S. Lewis
Waiting on God, Simone Weil
Butterflies *(illus.)*, E. B. Ford
Marx, David McLellan
Soft City, Jonathan Raban
Social Welfare in Modern Britain, edited by Butterworth &
Holman
Europe: Hierarchy and Revolt 1320-1450, George Holmes
Black Holes, John Taylor
The First Four Georges *(illus.)*, J. H. Plumb
Letters of Vincent Van Gogh *(illus.)*, edited by Mark Roskill
Food for Free *(illus.)*, Richard Mabey
Language Made Plain, Anthony Burgess

Edmund Burke
On Government, Politics and Society

Selected and Edited by B. W. Hill

Quoted more frequently than almost any other political writer, Edmund Burke has been cast in many roles – as arch-defender of established authority, radical critic of traditional orthodoxies, exponent of liberal values. Yet the historical Burke is a much more complex and fascinating thinker than any of these views allows.

The aim of this new selection is to reveal the range of Burke's outlook as politician, imaginative writer, and philosopher by drawing upon the extensive speeches and pamphlets on the American Colonies, the Monarchy and the Party system, and the Government of India, as well as the more widely known *Reflections on the Revolution in France*.

In his long introduction and editorial comments, Dr Hill presents Burke as an eclectic thinker, but a consistent advocate of social morality, a friend of good caring government, and an opponent of extremist politics whether of the Right or the Left.

'Almost alone in England, he brings thought to bear upon politics, he saturates politics with thought.'
Matthew Arnold

'Burke *is* an extraordinary man. His stream of mind is perpetual.'
Samuel Johnson

'No English writer has received, or has deserved, more splendid panegyrics than Burke.'
Leslie Stephen

'There is no wise man in politics, with an important decision to make, who would not do well to refresh his mind by discussion with Burke's mind.'
Harold Laski

Hitler: The Führer and the People

J. P. Stern

His life, his times, his policies, his strategies, his influence have often been analysed. But rarely is the most elementary question of all raised – how could it happen?

How could a predominantly sober, hard-working, and well-educated population have been persuaded to follow Hitler to the awful abyss of destruction? What was the source of his immense popularity? What was the image projected in his speeches, his writings, and his conversation?

Hitler: The Führer and the People is a compelling attempt to reconstruct the nature of Hitler's political ideology, its roots, logic, and function.

'Who really wants or needs another book on Hitler? The short answer is, when the book is as good and original and brief as Professor Stern's, that we all do.'
Donald G. MacRae, *New Statesman*

'Stern's book is, on all counts, a significant achievement.'
Geoffrey Barraclough, *New York Review of Books*

'. . . an excellent book, all the more so because it concerns itself, via Hitler, with the more general problems of the relationship between society and the individual leader, between ideas and action, between myth and reality.'
Douglas Johnson, *New Society*

'His short book is one of the most remarkable studies of Hitler and Nazism to have appeared.'   Christopher Sykes, *Observer*